$f\mathbf{P}$

Rabbi Jonathan Sacks

The Free Press
New York   London   Toronto   Sydney   Singapore

A
Letter
in the Scroll

Understanding
Our Jewish Identity
and Exploring the Legacy
of the World's Oldest Religion

THE FREE PRESS
A Division of Simon & Schuster Inc.
1230 Avenue of the Americas
New York, NY 10020

THE FREE PRESS and colophon are trademarks
of Simon & Schuster Inc.

Designed by Deirdre C. Amthor
Title page photograph of the Hurva Synagogue (Jewish Quarter, Old
City–Jerusalem) courtesy of Jonathon E. Brodman

Manufactured in the United States of America

10   9   8   7   6   5   4   3   2   1

Library of Congress Cataloging-in-Publication Data

Sacks, Jonathan, Rabbi.
A letter in the scroll: understanding our Jewish identity and exploring
the legacy of the world's oldest religion/Jonathan Sacks.
p. cm.
Includes bibliographical references and index.
1. Judaism—Essence, genius, nature. I. Title.

BM565.S217 2000   00-055157
296—dc21

ISBN 0-7432-0108-6

לזכר נשמת אבי מורי
ר׳ דוד אריה בן יהודה ז״ל
״וצדיק באמונתו יחיה״

ולהבדיל בין חיים לחיים
לבני בכורי אברהם יהודה
ולרעיתו חוה
״ישיש עליך אלוקיך כמשוש חתן על כלה״

To the memory of my late father, Louis David Sacks
And to our son Joshua and daughter-in-law Eve:
Our continuity

Contents

Preface

TODAY THROUGHOUT THE DIASPORA one Jew in two is either marrying out, or not marrying, or in some other way deciding not to create a Jewish home, have Jewish children, and continue the Jewish story.

At such moments—rare in our history—we, or our children, face the question, Who am I and why should I remain a Jew? That question can never be answered in the abstract. It is intensely personal and demands a personal reply.

This is my personal reply. None of us can answer this question for anyone else. But it sometimes helps to know how other people have thought about it, which is why I have decided to publish this book as an open letter to the next generation.

Writing it turned out to be, for me, a journey of discovery. Time and again as I asked, not What? but Why?, to my surprise I found Judaism disclosing itself to me in a way I had not seen before. So at the heart of the story I have to tell is my own theology of Judaism, something I have never previously written.

The more I penetrated into the mystery of Jewish survival, the more clearly I saw the originality, the distinctiveness, the sheer sanity of its vision of the world and of mankind, and how little it is understood by ourselves and others even now. We need to go back to our texts. Crisis is creative. It allows us—as more settled times do not—to encounter an ancient heritage afresh.

I presented the first draft of this book to our son Joshua and daughter-in-law Eve on the day of their wedding. It is my gift to them. It is also a tribute to my late father, of blessed memory, and to what I learned from him. This is my *yizkor*, my prayer to his memory. For when Jews remember, they do so for the future, the place where, if we are faithful to it, the past never dies.

Rosh Chodesh Elul 5760

A
Letter
in the Scroll

Prologue

A GROUP OF JEWISH UNIVERSITY STUDENTS had come to see me. They were planning their course for the next year and they wondered whether I could suggest a theme.

I thought for a moment and then I suggested this: There are many Jews today doing interesting and significant things. There are artists and academics, judges and doctors, politicians and heads of voluntary organizations, writers and journalists. Their work must raise, in a myriad ways, important questions about what to do and how to live. Write to them and ask them whether they would give you a brief personal statement about what being a Jew means to them and how it makes a difference to their lives. You will then have a series of texts that you will be able to compare with some of the classic statements of our tradition. You will be able to listen to the voices of the past and those of the present, and between them you can construct a fascinating series of discussions on what being a Jew might mean to you.

The students were excited by the suggestion, and during the weeks that followed we exchanged ideas about whom to ask and how to construct the questions. Months passed, and hearing no more about the project I inquired about its progress. They told me that they had sent out almost two hundred letters, and received only six replies. These were three of them. The first came from a famous and distinguished Jewish academic. He wrote:

> I am quite incapable of writing even a short passage on what being Jewish means to me. All that I think is that I am a Jew, in exactly the sense in which I have two legs, arms, eyes etc. It is just an attribute, which I take for granted as belonging to me, part of the minimum description of me as a person. I am neither proud of it nor embarrassed by it. I am just a Jew and it never occurred to me that I could be anything else. The question "Why be Jewish?" is something that I cannot answer any more than "Why be alive?" or "Why be two-legged?"

The second came from a noted Jewish writer:

> Jewishness is a source of comfort and reassurance to me and gives me a sense of belonging to a proud and ancient community, but all that is entirely due to the fact that I was brought up as a Jew. I have no doubt that I would have felt the same had I been brought up as a Catholic, Protestant, Muslim, Buddhist or Hottentot.

The third came from an Israeli, prominent in public life in Israel and the Diaspora:

> One of the most interesting definitions of Judaism that I know is something that I heard a number of years ago from a young Israeli boy. Judaism, he said, is

a hereditary illness. You get it from your parents, and also pass it along to your children. "And why call it an illness?" I asked. "Because not a small number of people have died from it," he answered.

The students felt let down, and to be honest, so did I. Here were three Jews, none of them hostile to Judaism or the Jewish people, two religiously committed and the third famous for his defense of some central Jewish values. Each had taken the trouble to write a message to the next generation. Yet the message itself was strangely ambivalent. For the first two, being Jewish was a mere accident of birth. For the third it was worse than an accident. It was an illness. The students felt, and I agreed, that there was nothing here on which a college course could be built.

So the next time I addressed a student group, I read them these responses. Then I asked them to listen to some other voices reflecting on Judaism and the Jewish people. I read to them these words by the great Russian novelist Leo Tolstoy:

> The Jew is that sacred being who has brought down from heaven the everlasting fire, and has illumined with it the entire world. He is the religious source, spring and fountain out of which all the rest of the peoples have drawn their beliefs and their religions.[1]

And these by the nineteenth-century American president John Adams:

> I will insist that the Hebrews have done more to civilize men than any other nation. If I were an atheist, and believed in blind eternal fate, I should still believe

that fate had ordained the Jews to be the most essential instrument for civilizing the nations. If I were an atheist of the other sect, who believe or pretend to believe that all is ordered by chance, I should believe that chance had ordered the Jews to preserve and propagate to all mankind the doctrine of a supreme, intelligent, wise, almighty sovereign of the universe, which I believe to be the great essential principle of all morality, and consequently of all civilization.[2]

I read them this passage by the contemporary historian Paul Johnson:

All the great conceptual discoveries of the intellect seem obvious and inescapable once they have been revealed, but it requires a special genius to formulate them for the first time. The Jews had this gift. To them we owe the idea of equality before the law, both divine and human; of the sanctity of life and the dignity of the human person; of the individual conscience and so of personal redemption; of the collective conscience and so of social responsibility; of peace as an abstract ideal and love as the foundation of justice, and many other items which constitute the basic moral furniture of the human mind. Without the Jews it might have been a much emptier place.[3]

And lastly this by the economist and former editor of *The Times* of London, William Rees-Mogg:

One of the gifts of Jewish culture to Christianity is that it has taught Christians to think like Jews, and any modern man who has not learned to think as though he were a Jew can hardly be said to have learned to think at all.[4]

These were astonishing accolades, and of course they were sympathetic voices. But the irony is that had I chosen *un*sympathetic voices—the writings of anti-Semites—they would have attributed even greater power to the Jews, whom they saw as exercising an almost total influence over the media, the economy and the politics of the West.

Here were conflicting testimonies, and reflecting on them I found myself in the presence of not one mystery but two: Who were and are this people who have exercised so great an influence on Western civilization? And why this strange contrast between what non-Jews and Jews have to say about them? Why was it that, while non-Jews saw in Jews and Judaism something extraordinary, Jews themselves went to such elaborate lengths to deny it, to claim the virtue of being ordinary as if it were a rare and special achievement? This much was clear to me: that there is confusion and demoralization at the heart of contemporary Jewish identity.

But there is also the hint of something vast and impressive. Another quotation came to mind, this time by the American-Jewish writer Milton Himmelfarb: "Each Jew knows how thoroughly ordinary he is; yet taken together, we seem caught up in things great and inexplicable . . . The number of Jews in the world is smaller than a small statistical error in the Chinese census. Yet we remain bigger than our numbers. Big things seem to happen around us and to us."[5]

What is it about this "thoroughly ordinary" people that

lifts it up, time and again, into "things great and inexplicable"? And why are so many Jews unaware of it? Without meaning to, I'd wandered into some of the most perplexing questions about Jewish existence, past and present. I discovered how hard it has become for Jews to say why they are Jews and why, if they do, they want the Jewish story to continue. That is what started me on a journey of self-discovery.

"People ask me why I am a Jew." It was with these words that the French writer Edmond Fleg began his book *Why I Am a Jew*, published in 1927.[6] More than seventy years later I felt the need to do the same.

Fleg wrote his book at a time when there were widespread defections from Judaism, and so have I. In many ages, questions like these would have been unnecessary. Our ancestors were Jews because their parents were Jews, and so were their parents, back across the centuries to ancient times. That is how Judaism and the Jewish people survived. In no small measure that is what it is to be a Jew— to inherit a faith from those who came before us, to live it, and to hand it on to those who will come after us. To be a Jew is to be a link in the chain of the generations.

But there are times when the chain begins to break, when the continuity of Judaism and the Jewish people can no longer be taken for granted. Fleg's was one; ours is another. At such moments, questions are unavoidable. Who are we? Of what story are we a part? Why were our ancestors so determined that it should continue? Does what spoke to them speak to us?

More than three thousand years ago, Moses made a request that has echoed down the ages. Speaking to the Israelites who were about to enter the promised land, he said,

"And you shall teach these things to your children, speaking of them when you are at home or on the way, when you lie down and when you rise up."[7] Moses was the leader of a small and injured people. They had been slaves; now they were free. They had set out on a long and tortuous journey through the desert, and they had not yet reached their destination.

They were not a people to inspire confidence. They were quarrelsome, ungrateful, indecisive and at times disloyal. Yet Moses sensed that something great had happened to them, something whose significance went far beyond that time, that place and this people. He believed—no, he *knew*—that this people would be the carriers of an eternal message, one that would have an effect not only on itself but on the civilization of the world. But only if successive generations of Jews took it upon themselves to hand down their beliefs to their children and their children's children.

Just before Moses said these words he made an even more poignant request: "You shall love the Lord your God with all your heart and with all your soul and with all your might."[8] The sixteenth-century commentator Rabbi Moses Alshekh was surely right when he said that these two verses are connected. We can only pass on to our children what we ourselves love.[9] We cannot order our children to be Jews. We cannot deprive them of their choice, nor can we turn them into our clones. All we can do is to show them what we believe, and let them see the beauty of how we live. As the English poet Wordsworth said: "What we love, others will love, and we will show them how."[10]

I cannot tell my children and grandchildren what they should be. Only they can make that choice, and I wish them blessing in whatever they decide. But I can tell them where we came from, and where our ancestors were traveling to, and why it was important to them that their children should carry on the journey. This is our story, unfinished yet. And there is a chapter only they can write.

Part I

The Question

1

Why Be Jewish?

SOMETIMES YOU CAN IDENTIFY the moment when a critical question is asked for the first time.

My journey into Jewish identity begins five hundred years ago in Spain, in a place called Calatayud, in the study of the rabbi of the town, Rabbi Isaac ben Moses Arama. He has already gained a wide reputation for his addresses, for they have broken new ground. They are not brief homilies but extended reflections on Jewish philosophy, which take off from some problem in the biblical portion of the week and then soar into the heights of theological speculation.

There is a sense of an ending, for the year is coming to a close. The Jewish New Year is at hand. We have reached the Torah portion of *Nitzavim* (near the end of the book of Deuteronomy) in which Moses, at the end of his life, renews the covenant of Sinai, some forty years later, with the members of the new generation:

> All of you are standing today in the presence of the Lord your God—your leaders and chief men, your elders and officials, and all the other men of Israel, together with your children and your wives, and the

aliens living in your camps who chop your wood and carry your water. You are standing here in order to enter into a covenant with the Lord your God, a covenant the Lord is making with you this day and sealing with an oath, to confirm you this day as His people, that He may be your God as He promised you and as He swore to your fathers, Abraham, Isaac and Jacob. I am making this covenant with its oath, not only with you who are standing here with us today in the presence of the Lord our God but also with those who are not here with us today.[1]

The words are familiar, but a question has occurred to him. Good! This is the way he usually starts a sermon. But as he searches for an answer, he finds himself becoming more enmeshed in perplexity. With a tremor he realizes that this is no ordinary question, for it threatens to unravel his entire life's work, and indeed his very identity. Eventually he finds an answer and delivers the sermon. But the question has not gone away.[2]

The question, as he eventually formulated it, was this: Moses stated that he was making the covenant not only with those who were there but also with those who were not there. To whom was he referring as not having been there? Clearly he did not mean members of the nation at that time. They were all there, as the text makes emphatically clear. Nor was he referring to the previous generation. They had already accepted the covenant at Mount Sinai. He meant, as Rashi explains, *those who are not yet born*—the generations to come.[3]

Hence the vital importance of this text. It is the very basis of Jewish destiny, the collective immortality of the people of Israel. The covenant will be eternal. It will bind all future generations. Jews will be born into its obligations. Each will be, in the talmudic phrase, *mushba ve-omed mi-Sinai*, "already forsworn at Sinai."[4] There is no need for assent, consent or confirmation. Converts excepted, Jews do not become Jews. They are Jews by birth. Jewish identity, then, is not only a faith, but a fate. It is not an identity we assume, but one into which we are born. That is the proper understanding of the passage as Jewish tradition, and Arama himself, had always read it.

For the first time, though, Arama saw a gap in the logical structure of the covenant. Obligation presupposes consent. I am bound by the promises I make, but I am not bound by the promises you make, unless I agree. There is a rule in Jewish law that someone can impose a benefit on another person without his knowledge. Because he gains, we can therefore assume his agreement. But by the same token someone cannot impose an obligation on another person without his knowledge, for there is no reason to assume that he would agree.[5] For that reason, children do not inherit their parents' debts unless property was explicitly mortgaged to meet them.

Now, undoubtedly it is a benefit to be born a Jew. But it is also very demanding. A Jew is bound by 613 commandments. There are restrictions and obligations that he would not have had were he not a Jew. Therefore we cannot impose this status on a person in his absence—without, that is to say, his explicit consent. But that is just what Moses was doing on the banks of the Jordan. He was asking the Israelites to bind their descendants, not yet born, to keep the covenant. That meant imposing obligations on them in their absence, without their agreement. How could one generation bind its successors? How could children be born into duties to which they had not given their consent? How was the eternity of the covenant morally possible?

The rabbi knew that there was a traditional answer, one that went back to an early rabbinical interpretation.[6] According to this, the souls of all future generations of Jews were present at Mount Sinai. They heard the voice of God. They witnessed revelation. They signaled their assent. But for the first time, Arama realized that this answer would not do.

He puts it this way: a person is a combination of body and soul—absent one, and personhood is lacking. Without a soul, the body is lifeless. Without a body, the soul floats in air. But the two experience the Torah differently. To the soul, God's command is a delight. To the body, it is a series of constraints. How then does it solve the problem to say that the souls of future generations accepted the Torah? Naturally they would. It is not the soul that might register an objection, but the body. If, then, future generations were not *physically* present at Mount Sinai we cannot take their agreement for granted. The moral agent—body and soul together—simply was not there. The mystical answer does not answer the moral question.

Isaac Arama eventually proposed a solution. But what has brought me back across the centuries to revisit him in his study that evening is this: that to my knowledge this was the first time the question had been asked in more than a thousand years. In essence Arama was raising the most fundamental of questions: *Why am I a Jew?* How can the mere fact that my parents were Jews obligate me? How can I be bound by a covenant enacted long ago in the desert by my distant ancestors? Though the vast literature of early and medieval rabbinic Judaism raises almost every conceivable issue, this one question is conspicuous by its absence. The very fact that a question of this kind is posed testifies to a crisis, because it calls into question something that at all other times is taken for granted.

For centuries Spain had been the home of medieval Jewry's golden age. Under relatively liberal regimes, Jews had risen to eminence in business, the sciences and public life. Their expertise was sought in finance, medicine and diplomacy. They sustained a rich intellectual and cultural life. Jewish learning flourished. Spanish Jewry was noted for its achievements in Jewish law, mysticism and philosophy. But the Jews of Spain were also well versed in the wider culture and made fine contributions to its poetry, politics, astronomy, medicine and cartography.

They were never totally secure. There were periodic attempts to convert them to Christianity. In 1263 the Jewish community was summoned to a public disputation. The Jewish spokesman, Nahmanides, successfully refuted the arguments of his opponent, but he had to pay a price. Two years later he was sentenced to exile. Then, in 1391, there was a volcanic explosion of anti-Jewish feeling. Throughout Spain there were riots. Synagogues were burned, houses and businesses were looted, and many Jews were killed.

For the first time, significant numbers of Jews converted to Christianity. For the next hundred years, there was wave after wave of conversionary activity, accompanied by anti-Jewish legislation. Jews who converted were offered equal citizenship. Those who remained Jewish were confined to special areas, forced to wear distinctive clothing, barred from public life and forbidden to mix with Christians. Eventually, in 1492, the remaining Jews were expelled.

There had been forced conversions before, under both Christian and Islamic rule, but never in such numbers or with such prominence. In the eleventh century Judah Halevi wrote in the *Kuzari* about the faithfulness of oppressed Jews who, "with a word lightly spoken," could have ended their misery by joining the faith of their oppressors.[7] In his day the number of converts was small, and he could speak with pride of the heroic resistance of most Jews, who preferred to stay Jewish and suffer rather than desert their faith for the sake of gain.

A century later, the picture was darker. Moses Maimonides, the greatest rabbi of the Middle Ages, was approached for advice by the Jewish community in Yemen. A fanatical Shi'ite Muslim movement was threatening to wipe out Jews who did not convert to Islam. Many did convert. What made things worse was that one of the converts—Samuel, son of Rabbi Judah ibn Abbas—became a missionary to the Jews. Harassed and demoralized, the community turned to Maimonides, who in 1172 replied in a long letter known as *The Epistle to Yemen*.[8]

He comforted the Jews who remained, telling them that "these trials are designed to test and purify us." In fact, he said, the Jews who converted were not really Jews, since "God has given assurance . . . that not only did all the persons who were present at the Sinaitic revelation believe in the prophecy of Moses and in his Law, but that their descendants would do so until the end of time."[9] Since all future generations had committed themselves at Mount Sinai, those who defected to another faith merely showed that they were not really Jews. They were not the true descendants of those who stood at Sinai.

So Halevi and Maimonides knew about Jews who left Judaism. They were called *conversos* or *anusim*, forced converts. But not until the mass conversions of fourteenth- and fifteenth-century Spain did the phenomenon provoke a crisis of faith within Jewry itself. Jews were leaving in great numbers. Many—*marranos*, as they came to be known—continued to practice Judaism in secret. Those who refused to make such a compromise saw their kinsmen held in honor while they were persecuted. So for the first time a question came to be asked: *Why* should I remain a Jew? Why should the mere fact that my parents were Jews obligate me to continue? Why should I suffer because of my faith?

We have evidence that these questions troubled the minds of even the most faithful Jews. Don Isaac Abrabanel, contemporary of Rabbi Arama, was the most distinguished Jew of his age. He had been treasurer to King Alfonso V of Portugal and a member of the court of Ferdinand and Isabella of Castile. He was also an outstanding Jewish scholar and wrote a great biblical commentary, still studied today. He lived through the Spanish expulsion and escaped to Naples, where he wrote a commentary to the Haggadah. In the course of this work he makes an extraordinary confession. There were moments during those tragic years when, he says, he came close to feeling that "all the Prophets who prophesied about my redemption and salvation are false.... Moses may he rest in peace was false in his utterances, Isaiah lied in his consolations, Jeremiah and Ezekiel lied in their prophesies, and likewise all the other prophets ... Let the people remember ... all the despairing things they used to say at the time of the Exile."[10] This tone of despair, too, is unprecedented in more than a thousand years.

When Jews ask the question "Why be Jewish?" we know that we are in the presence of a major crisis in Jewish life. I know of only four such occasions in Jewish history. The first occurred in the wake of the destruction of the first Temple in 586 B.C.E. In exile in Babylon, Jews might have gone the way of the ten tribes of the northern kingdom, who a century and a half earlier had assimilated and disappeared. The book of Ezekiel tells us that there were Jews who argued "We want to be like the nations, like the [other] peoples of the earth."[11] In other words, they no longer wanted to be Jews.

The second crisis occurred after the destruction of the second Temple and the later Hadrianic persecutions. A passage in the Babylonian Talmud states that "by rights we should issue a decree against ourselves not to get married and have children, so that the seed of Abraham comes to an end of its own accord."[12] So great are our sufferings that we should simply not bring any more Jews into the world. Another passage from the same period raises the following question: "If a master sells his slave, or a husband divorces his wife, does he then have any further claim on them?"[13] God had handed His people over to the Romans. He no longer ruled their destiny. He had failed to protect them from defeat and savage reprisals. By what right, then, could He lay claim to their loyalty? Why should they continue to be Jews?

The third occurred, as we have seen, in fifteenth-century Spain. For the first time Jews converted to another faith in significant numbers. Those who did so seemed to prosper. Those who remained loyal to their faith suffered ever-increasing persecution. In times such as those, what answer could rabbis like Arama and Abrabanel give to someone who asked, "Why should I remain a Jew?"

The fourth crisis has occurred in our time. For sixty years

Jews throughout Europe were the victims of a crescendo of anti-Semitism, culminating in the shattering tragedy of the Holocaust. Where was God when His people were being insulted, humiliated, attacked, degraded, and eventually rounded up and murdered in their millions? Elie Wiesel put it simply: "The Jewish people entered into a covenant with God. We were to protect His Torah and He in turn assumes responsibility for Israel's presence in the world . . . Well, it seems, for the first time in history, this very covenant is broken."[14] Wiesel was wrong in only one respect: it was not the first but the fourth time that the Jewish people had experienced this crisis.

From a Jewish perspective, crisis is experienced in the widespread feeling that the covenant between Israel and God has collapsed. God had promised that the Jewish people would survive. Four times in four thousand years it seemed that survival was in doubt. The Babylonian conquest, the Roman persecutions, the Spanish Expulsion and the Holocaust could easily have brought about the end of the Jewish people. In the first two instances, Jews lost their sovereignty. In the third, they lost their hope of finding security somewhere in the Diaspora. In the fourth, one-third of the Jewish people lost their lives.

What haunts us today, however, is that the fourth crisis did not end with the liberation of the camps and the conclusion of the Second World War. It continues in a new and troubling form. At present, throughout most communities in the Diaspora, one young Jew in two is in effect deciding not to continue the Jewish story by living a Jewish life, marrying another Jew, and having Jewish children and grandchildren. Jewish identity in the contemporary world is being transformed from fate to choice, from a fact of birth to a consciously chosen commitment; and significant numbers of young Jews are evidently unwilling to make that commitment. The future of the Jewish people is once again at risk, this time without the backdrop of external persecution. The question Why be Jewish? is being raised again in a new and searching form.

Judaism is a religion of continuity. It depends for its very existence on the willingness of successive generations to hand on their faith and way of life to their children, and on the loyalty of children to the heritage of their past. That is why the question is so rarely asked in Jewish history and why we have had to travel to fifteenth-century Spain to find a precedent. At most times Jews have seen themselves as a chosen, not a choosing, people. Their identity was self-evident, a given of birth; a fact, not a decision. So when in the past Jews asked why they should continue to be Jewish, what was the answer?

2

Answers

Isaac Arama gave one reply. After thousands of years, Jewish identity was as deeply engraved in the minds of Jews as the instinct of life is in all living creatures. It was, as it were, hardwired into their consciousness. It was no more possible for Jews collectively to desert the covenant than it was for a species to commit suicide. In human societies, even in some parts of the animal kingdom, there are individuals who commit suicide. But they are always the exceptions. Even lemmings go to their death to protect the species as a whole. Within all that lives, there is a desire for life, an instinct for survival. And for Jews that instinct is for Jewish survival. If to live is to love life, then to be a Jew is to love Jewish life.[1]

Abrabanel gave a different answer. Ever since Sinai, Jews had committed themselves to God. They were His servants—they belonged to Him and were His property. Until, therefore, God Himself released them from that agreement, they were His. They were bound to the covenant, and the choice to leave was not theirs. Until God said otherwise, they were still His people, his "treasured possession."[2]

But in the end, neither was satisfied with these answers.

Both Arama and Abrabanel were forced back to a more ancient reply—to the words spoken by Ezekiel two thousand
years before:

> You say: We want to be like the nations, like the
> peoples of the earth . . . But what you have in mind
> will never happen. As surely as I live, declares the
> Lord God, I will rule over you with a mighty hand and
> an outstretched arm and with outpoured wrath.[3]

The message Ezekiel was conveying was this: Jews might
try to assimilate, but they would never succeed. History
would conspire to prevent it. Jews would find that even
though they converted, they were still regarded as Jews.
That is what Arama and Abrabanel told the *marranos*, the
converted Jews. Arama said, "You will find no rest among
the gentiles, and your life will hang in the balance."[4] Abrabanel said that though they and their descendants "would
do all in their power to assimilate, they would not succeed.
They would still be called Jews against their own will and
would be accused of Judaizing in secret and be burnt at the
stake for it."[5]

As it happens, they were right. Those who converted to
Christianity while practicing Judaism in secret became tar-
gets of the Spanish Inquisition, which lasted well into the
eighteenth century. Many were indeed burned at the stake.
In fifteenth-century Spain a new and terrible doctrine made
its first appearance. Reinvented four centuries later, it became known as racial anti-Semitism. In Spain it was called
limpieza de sangre, "purity of blood." Jews who had converted were eventually barred from public office, not because of their religion but simply because they were Jews

by race. These laws remained in place in Spain until 1860.[6]

The same argument was mounted in the modern age. Moses Hess was the first writer to confront German anti-Semitism. His book *Rome and Jerusalem* (1862) was in fact published seventeen years before the term "anti-Semitism" had been coined. But already Hess recognized that, despite all their attempts to assimilate, to reform Judaism and to become more German than the Germans, Jews would still find themselves regarded as outsiders: "Even baptism itself does not save him from the nightmare of Jew-hatred."[7]

Tragically, he too was right. As in Spain, so in Germany, France, Austria—Jews who assimilated, even converted, were still hated. So Dreyfus discovered in France, and Heinrich Heine in Germany. Prejudice persisted, and merely changed its ground from religion to race. Jewish identity was, as Ezekiel had said, an inescapable fate. Those who tried to escape usually discovered as the prophet warned that "what you have in mind will never happen."

This, then, is the classic Jewish answer, and it has a tragic measure of historical truth. But it cannot suffice. Why? Firstly, because some Jews did in fact succeed in assimilating and disappearing. In the days of the first Temple, when Israel split into two and the northern kingdom was conquered by the Assyrians, ten of the twelve tribes mixed with the local population and ceased to exist as a distinct group. A historian has calculated that the Jews alive today are the children of a mere two percent of those who were alive in the days of the second Temple.[8] In ages of tolerance, Jews can cease to be Jews.

More important, though, Ezekiel's is a despairing vision, an answer of last resort. It sees Jewish existence as a matter of passive fate rather than active faith. Whatever we try to do, we will find that Jewish identity is inexorable. If we do not pursue it, it will pursue us.

This cannot be a complete answer because it fails to do justice to the proposition at the heart of Judaism: that God, who led His people from slavery to freedom, desires the free worship of free human beings. To be sure, there is a strange and famous statement in the Talmud that when God gave Israel the Torah He suspended Mount Sinai above their heads and said, "If you accept it, well and good. If not, this will be your burial place."[9] According to this, once Jews had been chosen, they had no choice but to accept the terms of Jewish life. However, the rabbis immediately rejected this idea. "If so, there is a fundamental objection to the Torah,"[10] for there can be no covenant without voluntary acceptance.

Judaism is a supreme expression of religion as freedom, and hence of the priority of faith over fate. Therefore I prefer to search for another answer, one truer to the central values of our faith. God calls on us to undertake a journey. He did so to Abraham and his family. He did so again to Moses and his people. They were free to decline. At many points along the way, they or those they led had doubts. But somehow the vision they saw was compelling—not because of its coercive force, its implacable fate, but by its moral beauty and spiritual grace.

I want to retrace that journey as best I can. Along the way I want to confront three questions. The first is: *Who am I?* What are the claims that Jewish identity makes upon me? How can a set of moral and spiritual values appear, not just as a vision or a way of life, but as a call to me in the first person singular? Essentially, this is the question Arama first asked. How can an ancient covenant still obligate the descendants of those who first made it? How can the past bind the present?

The second is: *Who are we?* What is the nature of the collective Jewish journey that I am asked to continue? What makes it different from other journeys, other faiths, other ways of relating to the world? And what makes it not just different but exhilarating, enlarging, a journey that, given the chance to take part in it, we would not lightly decline, not then and not now?

The third is: *How did we lose our way?* For if there is such a journey, and at least half of young Jews today are not choosing to take it, I want to understand why. Did they discover something previous generations did not know, that Judaism is less compelling, or other faiths more so, than our ancestors realized? Or did they simply lose something, the knowledge of what it is to be a Jew, and why?

Answering these questions means undertaking a journey. That is what Jewish identity has involved since the days of Abraham and Moses. It will not be straightforward—a Jewish journey never is. But it will be a journey through a whole series of radical and still not fully understood ideas. Along the way we will learn not only about what it is to be a Jew but also, and no less significantly, about what it is to be human. I have explained how Isaac Arama came to ask his question. This is how I came to ask mine.

3

Who Am I? Who Are We?

IT HAPPENED IN THE never-to-be-forgotten summer of 1967. I had just gone to university, leaving home for the first time. Until then I had been a Jew because—well, because that is what my parents were. I did what I did without asking why. I had my bar mitzvah, I went to Hebrew classes, and every Saturday I went to synagogue with my father. There was no reason not to, no reason to rebel.

Cambridge was like a revelation. Here for the first time I could feel the lure of another history, the siren call of a different culture. Everything about it was dazzling: the river, the lawns, the college buildings dating back to medieval times, the gowns, the bicycles, the dons, the whole rich texture of a world of stunning beauty that was not my own.

And there was an intellectual shock in store. Without quite intending to, I found myself studying philosophy—not the easiest of disciplines in which to preserve a religious faith. We were taught to study reality through language, and there was a lingering skepticism about the intelligibility of religious belief. One of the first books I read was A.J. Ayer's *Language, Truth and Logic*, a remarkable work written in the 1930s at the height of Logical Positivism, in which in a mere twenty pages he dismissed the whole of metaphysics, morals and religion as meaningless. If sentences were to make sense, he argued, they had to be testable either by logic or direct experience. Religion failed on both counts. You couldn't prove the existence of God. Nor could you experience a being who, by definition, lay beyond the physical world of the senses.[1]

The sixties were the years of liberation, when the young seemed to have all the answers, and the wisdom of the past, which once seemed so solid, turned out on closer inspection to be a cardboard facade that blew away in the wind. *The Times* of London, caught up in Beatlemania, compared the songs of Paul McCartney to German *lieder.* The distinguished Cambridge anthropologist Sir Edmund Leach, delivering the Reith Lectures on the BBC, announced that "far from being the basis of the good society, the family, with its narrow privacy and tawdry secrets, is the source of all discontents."[2] All the established conventions were crumbling before our eyes. Within a few years the liberal revolution confirmed what philosophy taught—that there were no rules, only preferences. Moral judgments were expressions of subjective emotion, not objective truths.

The university seemed like a microcosm of the universe. Here was every kind of student, from every kind of background, studying every subject in every conceivable way. What mattered was critical intelligence, the ability to question everything, accepting no answer on the basis of authority or age or tradition or revelation. Reality was confined to facts and inferences. Everything else was choice. You could be anything, do anything, intellectually and existentially. My parents' world seemed long ago and far away. These were heady days, and I was at the heart of it.

Then, in May, we began to hear disturbing news from the Middle East. The Egyptians had blocked the Gulf of Akaba. They demanded the withdrawal of the United Nations troops, who instantly complied. War was in the air. The State of Israel was exposed to attack on all fronts. A catastrophe seemed to be in the making. I, who had not lived through the Holocaust nor even thought much about it, became suddenly aware that a second tragedy might be about to overtake the Jewish people.

It was then that an extraordinary thing began to happen. Throughout the university Jews suddenly became visible. Day after day they crowded into the little synagogue in the center of town. Students and dons who had never before publicly identified as Jews could be found there praying. Others began collecting money. Everyone wanted to help in some way, to express their solidarity, their identification with Israel's fate. It was some time before we realized that the same phenomenon was repeating itself throughout the world. From the United States to the Soviet Union, Jews were riveted to their television screens or radios, anxious to hear the latest news, involved, on edge, as if it were their own lives that were at stake. The rest is history. The war was fought and won. It lasted a mere six days, one of the most spectacular victories in modern history. We could celebrate and breathe safely again. Life went back to normal.

But not completely. For I had witnessed something in those days and weeks that didn't make sense in the rest of my world. It had nothing to do with politics or war or even prayer. It had to do with Jewish identity. Collectively the Jewish people had looked in the mirror and said, We are still Jews. And by that they meant more than a private declaration of faith, "religion" in the conventional sense of the word. It meant that they felt part of a people, involved in its fate, implicated in its destiny, caught up in its tragedy, exhilarated by its survival. I had felt it. So had every other Jew I knew.

Why? The Israelis were not people I knew. They were neither friends nor relatives in any literal sense. Israel was a country two thousand miles away, which I had visited once but in which I had no plans to live. Yet I had no doubt that their danger was something I felt personally. It was then that I knew that being Jewish was not something private and personal but something collective and historical. It meant being part of an extended family, many of whose members I did not know, but to whom I nonetheless felt connected by bonds of kinship and responsibility.

It made no sense at all in the concepts and categories of the 1960s. That was when I first realized that being Jewish was an exceptionally odd thing to be, structurally odd. Jewish identity was not simply a truth or set of truths I could accept or reject. It was not a preference I could express or disavow. It was not a faith I could adopt or leave alone. I had not chosen it. It had chosen me. Everything I had studied in modern philosophy, everything I had experienced in contemporary culture, told me that truth was universal and all else was individual—personal preference, autonomous choice. But what I had experienced was neither universal nor individual. Jewish identity was not, nor did it aspire to be, the universal human condition. Nor had I chosen it. It was something I was born into. But how can anyone truly be born into specific obligations and responsibilities without their consent? Logically it didn't add up. Yet psychologically it did. Without any conscious decision I was reminded that merely by being born into the Jewish people I was enmeshed in a network of relationships that connected me to other people, other places, other times. I belonged to a people. And being part of a people, I belonged.

It didn't make sense in terms of twentieth-century thought. Yet it made eminent sense in the language of Jewish tradition. Rabbi Simeon bar Yochai, a teacher of the second century, had likened the Jewish people to a single body with a single soul: "When one of them is injured, they all feel pain."[3] The rabbis of that time defined the moral obligation behind the metaphor. They said, *Kol Yisrael arevim zeh bazeh*, "All Jews are responsible for one another."[4] And behind both of these statements was a much more ancient memory of the covenant undertaken by the Israelites in the desert at the foot of Mount Sinai in which they pledged themselves to a collective existence as a people under the sovereignty of God.

What I discovered in those emotional days of the summer of 1967—perhaps what each of us discovers when Jewish identity takes us by surprise—is that this covenant is still alive. It still had the power to move and transform me and my contemporaries—more power, perhaps, than any of us had suspected until then. But how? I was moved by curiosity to find out more about the horizontal links that bind Jews to one another and the vertical links binding us to a history and a hope. That was how I found myself asking the question Isaac Arama had asked five hundred years before. The search has taken up much of my life since then, because the question, once asked, does not go away.

Years after I left Cambridge, I found myself watching a television documentary about the great Egyptian temples. They had been built some three thousand three hundred years ago by the pharaoh assumed by most scholars to be the ruler at the time of the Exodus: Ramses II. Lovingly, the camera took us on a tour of those magnificent buildings, at Luxor, Karnak and Abu Simbel. The commentator spoke about their magnificence, their scale, their beauty, their sheer endurance across the millennia. They still stand, in little less than their former glory, defying time.

For twenty minutes or so I was carried along by his enthusiasm. Then I found myself asking what survives today of the Egypt of the pharaohs—the greatest, most powerful and by far the most long-lived of the empires of the ancient world? The buildings, the temples and the monuments remain, but not the people, the faith or the civilization. Already in the reign of Ramses II, the Egypt of the pharaohs had reached its peak. After his death it would begin its decline. By the time of the Alexandrian empire, ancient Egyptian culture had run its course. It had lasted many centuries, but like most other civilizations it had proved all too mortal. The stones remained; the world they celebrated was no more.

It occurred to me that among the builders of those temples must have been some of my ancestors. They were slaves in Egypt at the time. The Bible tells us that they were employed to build the cities of Pithom (Per-Atum) and Ramses, two of Ramses II's greatest projects. The contrast between the people and the king could not have been greater. The slaves were known as Hebrews, perhaps from the ancient word *Habiru*. They were, as the name implies, nomads, immigrants. They were *Ivrim*, meaning those who journey from place to place. In Egypt they had become slaves. They had no power, no wealth, no rights, no freedom. They were, of all people, the lowest of the low.

Egypt, at the time, was an indomitable power. Not only was it a country of immense technical prowess, but it ruled the entire region of the Middle East. Ramses was not so much served as a king; he was worshiped as a god. Colossal statues of him were to be found throughout the country.

The prefix *Ra* tells us that he was seen as the sun god. This explains an otherwise puzzling feature of the biblical story of the Exodus. The ten plagues that struck Egypt mounted in a rising scale of devastation, a sequence broken by the ninth, darkness, which seems less like an affliction than an inconvenience. The ninth plague, we now understand, was a judgment, not against the people but its most significant deity, the Pharaoh who saw himself as the god of the sun.

Suppose that we could travel back in time and tell the inhabitants of those days that it would not be the Egypt of the pharaohs, its empire and dynasty, that would survive. It would instead be that nation of slaves, known to others as Hebrews, to themselves as the children of Israel, and to later history as the Jews. Nothing would have struck them as more absurd. Indeed, the earliest known reference to the Israelites outside the Bible is an inscription on the Merneptah stele, a giant slab of black granite dating from the thirteenth century B.C.E. It reads, "Israel is laid waste. His seed is no more." Not only would the Egyptians not have believed that the people Israel would survive, they believed that they were already on the verge of extinction. Ancient Egypt and ancient Israel, therefore, seem to stand at opposite extremes of the great gamble we take with time. What endures and what wanes? What survives and what is eclipsed? It is a question we can never answer in advance, only in retrospect. But retrospect is what we have.

Egypt and Israel three millennia ago were nations that asked themselves the most fundamental human question of all: How do we defeat death and conquer mortality? How, in the brief span of a human life, do we participate in something that will endure long after we are no longer here? The Egyptians gave one answer—an answer that through the ages has tempted emperors and tyrants, rulers and kings.

We defeat mortality by building monuments that will stand for thousands of years. Their stones will outlive the winds and sands of time. The Jews gave an entirely different answer.

The Israelites, slaves in Egypt for more than two hundred years, were about to go free. Ten plagues had struck the country. Whatever their cause, they seemed to convey a message: The God of Israel is on the side of freedom and human dignity. On the brink of their release, Moses, the leader of the Jews, gathered them together and prepared to address them. He might have spoken about freedom. He could have given a stirring address about the promised land to which they were traveling, the "land flowing with milk and honey." Or he might have prepared them for the journey that lay ahead, the long march across the wilderness.

Instead, Moses delivered a series of addresses that seemed to make no sense in the context of that particular moment. He presented a new idea, revolutionary in character, whose implications remain challenging even now. He spoke about children, and the distant future, and the duty to pass on memory to generations yet unborn. Three times he turned to the theme:

> And when your children ask you, 'What do you mean by this rite?' you shall say . . . [5]

> And you shall explain to your child on that day, 'It is because of what the Lord did for me when I went free from Egypt.'[6]

> And when, in time to come, your child asks you, saying, 'What does this mean?' you shall say to him . . . [7]

About to gain their freedom, the Israelites were told that they had to become a nation of educators.

Freedom, Moses suggested, is won, not on the battlefield, nor in the political arena, but in the human imagination and will. To defend a land, you need an army. But to defend freedom, you need education. You need families and schools to ensure that your ideals are passed on to the next generation, and never lost, or despaired of, or obscured. The citadels of liberty are houses of study. Its heroes are teachers, its passion is education and the life of the mind. Moses realized that a people achieves immortality not by building temples or mausoleums, but by engraving their values on the hearts of their children, and they on theirs, and so on until the end of time.

The Israelites built living monuments—monuments to life—and became a people dedicated to bringing new generations into being and handing on to them the heritage of the past. Their great institutions were the family and education via the conversation between the generations. In place of temples they built houses of prayer and study. In place of stones they had words and teachings. They saw God not as the power that enslaves but as the power that sets free. Instead of worshiping mighty rulers they affirmed the dignity of the widow, the orphan, the stranger, the vulnerable, the weak and the neglected. In that counterintuitive reversal they discovered the secret of eternity. Whether through accident or design or something greater than either, the Hebrew slaves who built Ramses' temples had lived through one of the great revelations of history. These were our ancestors, and we are their heirs.

. . .

Was I right or wrong to see in this story something out of the ordinary? Only later did I discover that three other people, none of them Jews, had shared my own sense of amazement and had been persuaded by it that somewhere in the tale of Jewish survival was a mystery of great significance. Each of them, for different reasons, had been led to reflect on the nature of history. Each had been startled into a discovery that there was one people whose history broke all the rules.

The first was Blaise Pascal, a mathematician and physicist in the seventeenth century who invented the first digital calculator and the syringe, and discovered Pascal's law of pressure and the principle of the hydraulic press. More significantly, he was the founder of the modern theory of probability. At the age of thirty he abruptly ended his scientific work and devoted the rest of his life to thinking about religious faith. His theological reflections led him to formulate what has come to be known as "Pascal's wager," the idea that under conditions of uncertainty we have more to lose by disbelieving than by believing in God. However, Pascal also applied the idea of probability to history and came to a striking conclusion: that among all the myriad peoples that have lived on earth, only one defies probability:

> It is certain that in certain parts of the world we can see a peculiar people, separated from the other peoples of the world, and this is called the Jewish people . . . This people is not only of remarkable antiquity but has also lasted for a singularly long time . . . For whereas the peoples of Greece and Italy, of Sparta, Athens and Rome, and others who came so much later have perished so long ago, these still exist, despite the efforts of so many powerful kings who have tried a hundred times to wipe them out, as their historians

testify, and as can easily be judged by the natural order of things over such a long spell of years. They have always been preserved, however, and their preservation was foretold . . . My encounter with this people amazes me . . .[8]

In *War and Peace* Leo Tolstoy also wrestled with the question of the meaning of history. Is the course of events determined by the decisions of great leaders and military commanders? Or is there some deeper underlying thread of meaning, a destiny whose outline can be discerned beneath the surface of apparently random happenings? Critics have often been irritated by Tolstoy's philosophizing, which cuts across the vivid drama of the novel, the fate of five aristocratic families set against the panoramic background of Napoleon's invasion of Russia. Yet Tolstoy was driven by a conviction that there is a moral and spiritual dimension to history, and this idea left him no peace. At the height of his career, having completed *Anna Karenina*, he abandoned his life as an aristocrat and started living the life of a peasant, devoted to faith, love, and the virtues of simplicity. One of the things that, for him, proved the existence of a mysterious and providential pattern in history was the story of the Jews:

> He whom neither slaughter nor torture of thousands of years could destroy, he whom neither fire nor sword nor inquisition was able to wipe off the face of the earth, he who was the first to produce the oracles of God, he who has been for so long the guardian of prophecy, and who has transmitted it to the rest of the world—such a nation cannot be destroyed. The Jew is as everlasting as eternity itself.[9]

The third figure, Nicolay Berdyayev, was one of the great thinkers of the Russian Revolution. The destiny of civilizations, he believed, was ruled by material forces, economies, wars, the physical indices of power. Something happened, though, to make him change his mind. In his study of history he came across one people whose fate could not be accounted for in these terms—the Jewish people. Their existence and survival was a refutation of Marxist theory. This discovery changed Berdyayev's life. He became religious. He no longer believed in materialism but instead in the "light which breaks through from the transcendent world of the spirit." Eventually, he was expelled from Russia and spent the rest of his life in Berlin and Paris, teaching religion. In *The Meaning of History,* he tells how he made his discovery:

> I remember how the materialist interpretation of history, when I attempted in my youth to verify it by applying it to the destinies of peoples, broke down in the case of the Jews, where destiny seemed absolutely inexplicable from the materialistic standpoint . . . Its survival is a mysterious and wonderful phenomenon demonstrating that the life of this people is governed by a special predetermination, transcending the processes of adaptation expounded by the materialistic interpretation of history. The survival of the Jews, their resistance to destruction, their endurance under absolutely peculiar conditions and the fateful role played by them in history: all these point to the particular and mysterious foundations of their destiny.[10]

Here were three people whose lives were changed by their encounter with the Jewish story. Judaism confirmed their own religious faith and suggested to them the important idea that God might be found not only in nature but in history. And if we search for revelation in history, we will find it, more compellingly than anywhere else, in the history of that unusual people, our ancestors. For almost two thousand years Jews remained a distinctive nation without any of the usual prerequisites of nationhood. They had no land, no sovereignty, no power, no overarching political structures, not even a shared culture. They were scattered over the face of the earth, and almost everywhere they were a minority. For the most part, they refused active efforts to convert them and resisted the passive pull of assimilation. No other people kept its identity intact for so long in such circumstances.

And so I came back to the question that had perplexed me in my student days, and five centuries earlier had troubled Rabbi Isaac Arama. I was heir to this history. But what claim did it lay on me? In what sense did it represent my own identity, not as a fact but as a value, not as the story of a past but as a duty to the future? With this I come to the first of the three questions I want to answer: *How does where I come from tell me who I am called on to be?*

4

A Letter in the Scroll

THE HOLIEST OBJECT IN JUDAISM is a Sefer Torah, a scroll of
the law. Still written today as it was thousands of years ago,
by hand with a quill on parchment, it symbolizes some of
Judaism's deepest beliefs: that God is to be found in words,
that these words are to be found in the Torah, and that they
form the basis of the covenant—the bond of love—between
God and the Jewish people.

I wonder if any people has ever loved a book as we love
the Torah. We stand when it passes as if it were a king. We
dance with it as if it were a bride. If it is desecrated or destroyed, we bury it as if it were a relative or friend. We study
it endlessly as if in it were hidden all the secrets of our being. Heinrich Heine once called the Torah the "portable
homeland" of the Jewish people,[1] by which he meant that
when we lacked a land, we found our home in the Torah's
words. More powerfully still, the Baal Shem Tov—founder
of the Hassidic movement in the eighteenth century—said
that the Jewish people is a living Sefer Torah, and every Jew
is one of its letters. I am moved by that image, and it invites
a question—*the* question: Will we, in our lifetime, be letters
in the scroll of the Jewish people?

At some stage, each of us must decide how to live our

lives. We have many options, and no generation in history has had a wider choice. We can live for work or success or wealth or fame or power. We can have a whole series of lifestyles and relationships. We can explore any of a myriad of faiths, mysticisms, or therapies. There is only one constraint—namely, that however much of anything else we have, we have only one life, and it is short. How we live and what we live for are the most fateful decisions we ever make.

We can see life as a succession of moments spent, like coins, in return for pleasures of various kinds. Or we can see our life as though it were a letter of the alphabet. A letter on its own has no meaning, yet when letters are joined to others they make a word, words combine with others to make a sentence, sentences connect to make a paragraph, and paragraphs join to make a story. That is how the Baal Shem Tov understood life. Every Jew is a letter. Each Jewish family is a word, every community a sentence, and the Jewish people at any one time are a paragraph. The Jewish people through time constitute a story, the strangest and most moving story in the annals of mankind.

That metaphor is for me the key to understanding our ancestors' decision to remain Jewish even in times of great trial and tribulation. I suspect they knew that they were letters in this story, a story of great risk and courage. Their ancestors had taken the risk of pledging themselves to a covenant with God and of thus undertaking a very special role in history. They had undertaken a journey, begun in the distant past and continued by every successive generation. At the heart of the covenant is the idea of *emunah*, which means faithfulness or loyalty. And Jews felt a loyalty to generations past and generations yet unborn to continue the narrative. A Torah scroll that has a missing letter is rendered invalid, defective. I think that most Jews did not want theirs to be that missing letter. What, then, has changed? Why is this claim of loyalty to the past and future no longer self-evident to many young Jews? The answer, I believe, lies in one of the great confrontations between Judaism and modern thought.

Judaism is an iconoclastic faith that has, not once but many times, challenged the assumptions of an age, and it is hard, centuries later, to recapture the drama of those encounters. For us it is all too obvious why Abraham believed in one God, or why Moses fought against the enslavement of his people, or why the prophets battled against the corruption of public life. We are heir to their achievements; we see the world through their eyes and find it difficult to understand how people could have thought otherwise. History is the past as seen through the eyes of the victors, and Jews won a whole series of moral victories. As Thomas Cahill points out in his *The Gifts of the Jews*, to a large degree, Western civilization is framed in terms of concepts first articulated by the Jews.[2]

At the time, however, those victories were anything but inevitable. To the contrary, they called into question the foundational certainties of their age. The spiritual vision of the heroes and heroines of Jewish life was, when first formulated, angular, counterintuitive and strange. Not by accident did Moses, Isaiah and Jeremiah complain that they found it hard to speak the word of God. They meant that they found it difficult to say words that could be understood by their contemporaries; nor were they the last to do so. Judaism is God's perennial question mark against the conventional wisdom of mankind, and this has been the fate of Jewish identity in modern times. It belongs to a language, a way of seeing and thinking, that has become hard to translate into the concepts of today.

Several centuries of Western thought, beginning in the Enlightenment, have left us with the idea that when we choose how to live, we are on our own. Nothing in the past binds us. We are whoever and whatever we choose to be. So axiomatic is this idea to us that we are all too unaware of the intellectual history that lies behind it. We can trace some of the key moments: when David Hume in the eighteenth century stated that one could not derive an "ought" from an "is," or when Kant placed the concept of autonomy at the heart of the moral life, or when the twentieth-century existentialist Jean-Paul Sartre argued that for each of us, "existence precedes essence." This long, cumulative development has left us with the belief that identity is something we choose, unfettered by any bonds with the past. No fact defines our obligations, no history prescribes our roles. We enter the world with a clean slate on which we can draw any self-portrait we wish.

Against this whole complex of ideas, Jewish life is a sustained countervoice. To be a Jew is to know that this cannot be the full story of who I am. A melody is more than a sequence of disconnected notes. A painting is something other than a random set of brushstrokes. The part has meaning in terms of its place within the whole, so that if history has meaning, then the lives that make it up must in some way be joined to one another as characters in a narrative, figures in an unfolding drama. Without this it would be impossible to speak about meaning; and Judaism is the insistence that history *does* have a meaning. Therefore each of us has significance precisely insofar as we are part of a story, an extraordinary and exemplary story of a people dedicated to certain ideas. We are not free-floating atoms in infinite space. We are letters in the scroll.

One way of dramatizing the contrast is to imagine that we

are in a vast library. In every direction we look there are bookcases. Each has shelves stretching from the floor to the ceiling, and every shelf is full of books. We are surrounded by the recorded thoughts of many people, some great, some less so, and we can reach out and take any book we wish. All we have to do is choose. We begin to read, and for a while we are immersed in the world, real or imaginary, of the writer. It may intrigue us enough to lead us to look for other books by the same writer, or perhaps others on the same subject. Alternatively, we can break off and try a different subject, a different approach; there is no limit. Once the book no longer interests us, we can put it back on the shelf, where it will wait for the next reader to pick it up. It makes no claim on us. It is just a book.

That, for the contemporary secular culture of the West, is what identity is like. We are browsers in the library. There are many different ways of living, and none exercises any particular claim on us. None of them more than any other defines who we are, and we can try any for as long as we like. As browsers, though, we remain intact, untouched. The various lifestyles into which we enter are like books we read. We are always free to change them, put them back on the shelf. They are what we read, not what we are.

Judaism asks us to envisage an altogether different possibility. Imagine that, while browsing in the library, you come across one book unlike the rest, which catches your eye because on its spine is written the name of your family. Intrigued, you open it and see many pages written by different hands in many languages. You start reading it, and gradually you begin to understand what it is. It is the story each generation of your ancestors has told for the sake of the next, so that everyone born into this family can learn where they came from, what happened to them, what they lived for and why. As you turn the pages, you reach the last, which carries no entry but a heading. It bears your name.

According to the intellectual conventions of modernity, this should make no difference. There is nothing in the past that can bind you in the present, no history that can make a difference to who you are and who you are free to be. But this cannot be the whole truth. Were I to find myself holding such a book in my hands, my life would already have been changed. Seeing my name and the story of my forebears, I could not read it as if it were just one story among others; instead, reading it would inevitably become, for me, a form of self-discovery. Once I knew that it existed, I could not put the book back on the shelf and forget it, because I would now know that I am part of a long line of people who traveled toward a certain destination and whose journey remains unfinished, dependent on me to take it further.

With that newfound knowledge, I could no longer see the world simply as a library. Other books may make no special claim on me; they may be interesting, inspiring, entrancing, but this one is different. Its very existence poses a set of questions addressed, not to the universe, but to me. Will I write my own chapter? Will it be a continuation of the story of those who came before? Will I, when the time comes, hand the book on to my children, or will I by then have forgotten it or given it away to a museum as an heirloom from the past?

This is more than an imaginative exercise. There is such a book, and to be a Jew is to be a life, a chapter, in it. This book contains the knowledge of who I am and is perhaps the most important thing I can be given. Each of us, to feel we belong, needs to know something about our personal history—about who gave birth to us, where they came from, and the history of which they are a part. We see this most acutely in cases where, for whatever reason, this knowledge is missing. A child who is adopted almost invariably develops a curiosity about who its natural parents were, a curiosity that in some cases can amount to an obsession. The same is true about children abandoned by a parent before they were able to develop a relationship. Not to know who I am can be unnerving and lead to a sense of incompleteness. The question of identity is fundamental and cannot be answered without knowing that a certain definite past is mine.

We are, each of us, many things—part of this country, that region, this neighborhood, that group. We have friendships, commitments, passions and concerns that contribute to our personalities, but cannot substitute for the core of identity. I may be a lawyer, concerned about the environment; an American citizen living in Seattle who loves the films of Steven Spielberg and the humor of Woody Allen. But these are merely facts about me—what I do, what I care about, where I live, what I like—and they fall short of constituting *who I am*. They may change over time without my ceasing to be me. The most fundamental answer to the question "Who am I?"—the one that never changes—involves a journey back through time into who my parents were, and theirs, and so on as far back as I can go. That is the story into which I was born. I may choose not to continue it, but I cannot deny it without in some way living a lie. The history of my family is where my identity begins.

Unexpectedly, this most modern of questions has a biblical echo. The first question Moses asked of God was *mi anokhi*, "Who am I?" On the surface, this was an expression of doubt as to his personal worthiness to lead the Israelites to freedom. But there is also an echo of an identity crisis, rare in those days though all too familiar now. Who, after all, was Moses? A child hidden in a basket of reeds, found and adopted by an Egyptian princess, given an Egyptian name and brought up in Pharaoh's palace. Many years later, when circumstances force him to leave Egypt and take flight to Midian, he comes to the rescue of Jethro's daughters, who tell their father, "An Egyptian man delivered us." Moses looked, spoke and dressed like an Egyptian. Yet the text tells us that when he grew up he "went out to his brothers and saw their burdens." Somehow he knew that the enslaved Israelites were "his brothers." By upbringing he was an Egyptian; by birth he was a Jew.

The mind reels at such a choice. On the one hand lay a life of ease, position and power as a prince in Pharaoh's court; on the other, the prospect of years of struggle and privation as a member of a nation of slaves. Yet when God tells him, "I am the Lord, the God of your fathers, the God of Abraham, the God of Isaac and the God of Jacob," Moses' crisis is resolved and never reappears in that form. He now knows that he is part of an unfinished story that began with the patriarchs and continues through him. He may wear the clothes and speak the language of an Egyptian, but he is a Jew because that is who his ancestors were, and their hopes now rest on him. The modern Jewish question is unusual but not unprecedented: we are each faced with Moses' choice. By culture and upbringing we are part of the liberal democracies of the West, but by birth each of us is heir to the history of our ancestors and a destiny that joins our fate to theirs. There is a difference between *where* we are and *who* we are. Judaism was not wrong to see identity as a matter of birth, however deeply that cuts against the grain of post-Enlightenment culture.

The fact that any of us is born a Jew is no mere fact. It happened because more than a hundred generations of our ancestors decided to be Jews and hand on that identity to their children, thus writing the most remarkable story of continuity ever known. Nor was this mere happenstance. It flowed from their most basic conviction, that Jews had entered into a covenant with God that would take them on a journey whose destination lay in the distant future but whose outcome was of immense consequence for mankind. What that journey was would be the subject of the next part of my search, but one thing was clear from the outset. It would not be completed instantly. Unlike almost every other vision of the ideal society, Jews knew that theirs was the work of many generations and that therefore they must hand on their ideals to their children so that they too would be part of the journey, letters in the scroll. To be a Jew, now as in the days of Moses, is to hear the call of those who came before us and know that we are the guardians of their story.

At the end of his life the great non-Jewish literary historian A. L. Rowse published his memoirs, and at the end of the book he wrote a surprising sentence: "If there is any honour in all the world that I should like, it would be to be an honorary Jewish citizen."[3] That was his unfulfilled dream, but for those born into the story, it is not a dream but a birthright. We have inherited the book our ancestors wrote, and there is a letter that only we can write.

I am a Jew because, knowing the story of my people, I hear their call to write the next chapter. I did not come from nowhere; I have a past, and if any past commands anyone, this past commands me. I am a Jew because only if I remain a Jew will the story of a hundred generations live on in me. I continue their journey because, having come this far, I may not let it and them fail. I cannot be the missing letter in the scroll. I can give no simpler answer, nor do I know of a more powerful one.

Part II

The Journey

5

A Palace in Flames

ALMOST FOUR THOUSAND YEARS AGO, at the dawn of the history of our people, two people set off on a journey. They did not know where it would lead. All they knew was that they had heard a voice:

> *Leave your land, your birthplace and your father's house*
> *And go to the land I will show you.*
> *I will make you into a great nation.*
> *I will bless you and make you great.*
> *You shall become a blessing.*
> *I will bless those that bless you,*
> *And those who curse you, I will curse.*
> *All the families of the earth will be blessed through you.*[1]

Those were the words, and they were enough to set Abraham and Sarah off on a journey that would eventually change the world.

Where were they going, and what was it that they were about to do? The place they were going—the land of Canaan, later to become the land of Israel—was a small country midway between two great empires, Mesopotamia in the east and Egypt in the west. The life the couple led had no great public dramas. They longed for a child and eventually had one. They were caught up in the events of their time: famines, local battles, the destruction of the cities of the plain. But they were not heroic figures of the kind we find in Greek legends. Abraham was not a king or a warrior, a man of superhuman strength. For the most part, he and Sarah lived quietly, far from the arenas of power and fame.

What was special about them was that they had the courage to be different. They did not worship the idols of their time, but instead pledged their loyalty to the one God, creator of heaven and earth. When their neighbors were threatened, they prayed for them and fought for them. But they did not live like their neighbors. They had their own values. They kept to "the way of God, doing charity and justice."[2] This was the way they taught the members of their household and their son Isaac. Unlike those around them, they did not worship nature or power, they did not believe that the world was simply an arena of blind and clashing forces, and they rejected the myths and pagan practices of their time. As later tradition put it, "The whole world was on one side, and they were on the other."[3] There were times when their faith was put to the test, but they persevered, staying true to the voice they had heard.

▸ Jews were always a tiny people, yet our ancestors survived by believing that eternity is found in the simple lives of ordinary human beings. They found God in homes, families and relationships. They worshiped God in synagogues, the first places ever to become holy because of the mere fact that people gathered there to pray. They discovered God in the human heart and in our capacity to make the world different by what we do. They encountered God, not in the wind or the thunder or the earthquake, but in words, the words of Torah, the marriage contract between God and the people He took as His own. They studied those words endlessly and tried to put them into practice. They brought heaven down to earth, because they believed that God lives wherever we dedicate our lives to Him.

And somehow that small people did great things. They produced some of the greatest visionaries the world has ever known. They transformed the civilization of the West, teaching it to abandon myth and magic and see human history as the long, slow journey to freedom and justice. Nor did they flourish once and then decline. At each phase in their history they discovered new modes of spirituality. Prophets and priests were succeeded by scribes and sages, and then by commentators, jurists, poets, philosophers, mystics, and eventually by pioneers of the return to Zion.

When the gates of wider culture were opened to them, within the space of one or two generations Jews had produced from their ranks scientists, statesmen, financiers, businessmen, intellectuals and literati. They did so in medieval Spain. They did so again as Enlightenment dawned. They contributed an astonishing number of the makers of the modern mind. And when the gates were closed and the Jewish mind turned inward, its creative pulse hardly missed a beat as it directed its energies to Jewish law and piety and mystic speculation. Surrounded by poverty, ignorance and superstition, Jews sustained a life of literacy and religious scholarship. In Hamlet's phrase, their kingdom might be bounded by a nutshell, but they counted themselves kings of infinite space.

From the days of Moses, the people of Israel knew that their strength would not lie in numbers. "The Lord did not set His affection on you and choose you because you were more numerous than other peoples, for you are the fewest of all peoples."[4] Yet they held firm to the belief that God had a purpose for humanity and that the Jewish people had a unique role in bringing it about. They were, in some obscure but unmistakable way, "God's witnesses."[5] Their lives would reflect His will. Their history would reflect His plan. The relationship between God and Israel was sometimes tempestuous, often strained, but never broken. The Jewish people would be the bearers of God's presence in a sometimes godless, often unjust and violent world. In eras that worshiped the collective—the nation, the state, the empire—they spoke about the dignity and sanctity of the individual. In cultures that celebrated the right of the individual to do his or her own thing, they spoke of law and duty and mutual responsibility.

They were the first people in history to moralize power, to insist on the supremacy of right over might and on the authority of a prophet to criticize a king. They believed that though a vast distance separates the infinity of God from the finitude of man, something unites us, the moral enterprise of perfecting the world, in respect of which we are "partners of the Holy One, blessed be He, in the work of creation."[6] No people has insisted, so strenuously and consistently, on the overarching sovereignty of the moral imperative. As Paul Johnson has written: "The Jewish vision became the prototype for many similar grand designs for humanity, both divine and man-made. The Jews, therefore, stand right at the center of the perennial attempt to give human life the dignity of a purpose."[7]

Tradition offers several explanations of how the journey of Abraham and Sarah to an unknown destination began. According to one, Abraham was the iconoclast who broke his father's idols.[8] According to another, he was the philosopher who, seeing people worship the sun and the stars, asked "But who created *them?*" and thus arrived at the cause of causes, monotheism's one God.[9] But there is a third and altogether more radical reading. It comes from the literature of rabbinic commentary that we call *midrash*. According to this, Abraham's faith did not begin with an answer but with a question:

> "The Lord said to Abram: Leave your land, your birthplace and your father's house . . . " To what may this be compared? To a man who was traveling from place to place when he saw a palace in flames. He wondered, "Is it possible that the palace lacks an owner?" The owner of the palace looked out and said, "I am the owner of the palace." So Abraham our father said, "Is it possible that the world lacks a ruler?" The Holy One, blessed be He, looked out and said to him, "I am the ruler, the Sovereign of the universe."[10]

This is a deeply enigmatic passage, so much so that distinguished Jewish thinkers in our time have often misunderstood it. One of them translated the phrase "a palace in flames" as "a palace full of light."[11] According to this interpretation, Abraham was seized by a mystic vision of the beauty of the universe and found God in the light within the light. Another theologian interpreted it as an early form of what later became known as the "argument from design."[12] Beneath its apparent randomness, the universe discloses an intricate order. The world did not come about by chance. To be sure, at every stage, chance—random genetic mutation—played a part. But the outcome was the emergence of intelligent, self-conscious life. In retrospect we can see that this was the end to which evolution was tending despite the thousand improbabilities that accompanied every stage of the process. According to this reading, Abraham looked through the flames of chance and saw the palace of order, and there he found God, the owner of the palace who speaks to man.

These are both beautiful interpretations, and each has its own validity, but they are not true to the passage itself. Abraham sees a palace. The world has order, and therefore it has a creator. But the palace is in flames. The world is full of *dis*order, of evil, violence and injustice. Now, no one builds a building and then deserts it. If there is a fire, there must be someone to put it out. The building must have an owner. If so, where is he? That is the question, and it gives Abraham no peace.

With this we arrive at the starting point of Jewish faith, radical then, radical now, perhaps still not fully understood. Faith is born not in the answer but in the question, not in harmony but in dissonance. If God created the world, then He created man. Why then does He allow man to destroy the world? How are we to reconcile the order of nature with the disorder of society? Can God have made the world only to abandon it?

From time immemorial to the present, there have always been two ways of seeing the world. The first says, There is no God. There are contending forces, chance and necessity, the chance that produces variation, and the necessity that gives the strong victory over the weak. From this perspective, the evolution of the universe is inexorable and blind; there is no justice and no judge, and therefore there is no question. We can know *how*, but we can never know *why*, for there is no why. There is no palace. There are only flames.

The second view insists that there is God. All that is exists because He made it. All that happens transpires because He willed it. Therefore all injustice is an illusion. Perhaps the world itself is an illusion. When the innocent suffer, it is to teach them to find faith through suffering, obedience through chastisement, serenity through acceptance, the soul's strength through the body's torments. Evil is the cloak that masks the good. There is a question, but there is always an answer, for if we could understand God we would know that the world is as it is because it would be less good were it otherwise. There is a palace. Therefore there are no flames.

The faith of Abraham begins in the refusal to accept either answer, for both contain a truth, and between them there is a contradiction. The first accepts the reality of evil, the second the reality of God. The first says that if evil exists, God does not exist. The second says that if God exists, evil does not exist. But supposing both exist? Supposing there are both the palace and the flames?

If this is so and I have interpreted the *midrash* correctly, then Judaism begins not in wonder that the world is, but in protest that the world is not as it ought to be. It is in that cry, that sacred discontent, that Abraham's journey begins. At the heart of reality is a contradiction between order and chaos, the order of creation and the chaos we create. There is no resolution to this conflict at the level of thought. It can be resolved only at the level of action, only by making the world other than it is. When things are as they ought to be, *then* we have reached our destination. But that is not now: it was not now for Abraham, nor is it yet for us.

The easy answer would be to deny the reality of either God or evil. Then the contradiction would disappear and we could live at peace with the world. But to be a Jew is to have the courage to refuse easy answers and to reject either consolation or despair. God exists; therefore life has a purpose. Evil exists; therefore we have not yet achieved that purpose. Until then we must travel, just as Abraham and Sarah traveled, to begin the task of shaping a different kind of world.

Judaism is a uniquely restless faith. Jews are always traveling, dissatisfied with the status quo and never quite merging with their environment. The *midrash* suggests where and how these traits began. For Judaism, faith is cognitive dissonance, the discord between the world that is and the world as it ought to be. That tension has been the energizing mainspring of Jewish life from the time of Abraham to today.

What haunts us about the *midrash* is not just Abraham's question but God's reply. He gives an answer that is no answer. He says, in effect, "I am here," without explaining the flames. He does not attempt to put out the fire. It is as if, instead, He were calling for help. God made the building. Man set it on fire, and only man can put out the flames. Abraham asks God, "Where are you?" God replies, "I am here, where are you?" Man asks God, "Why did You abandon the world?" God asks man, "Why did you abandon Me?" So begins a dialogue between earth and heaven that has no counterpart in any other faith, and which has not ceased for four thousand years. In these questions, which only the other can answer, God and man find one another. Perhaps only together can they extinguish the flames.

What is morality? To this question there have traditionally been two answers. The first is that morality is objective. It is out there in the world of facts, in nature ("natural law") or in the structure of society and its generally accepted conventions. In this view, to be moral is to conform.

The second view is that morality is subjective. It is "in

here," in personal emotion, private desire, or inner intuition. There is no moral truth beyond that which we feel in our own hearts. According to this view, to be moral is to be true to yourself.

Adherence to either of these views has yielded disastrous results. Nature is often blind and cruel, societies have been oppressive and conventions have been unjust. Sometimes morality demands that we do not conform. But if we are only true to ourselves, then we buy our freedom at the expense of others. Desires conflict, as do emotions and intuitions. Societies built on the principle of each doing "that which is right in his own eyes" end in violence and manipulation.

For Judaism, morality is something else. It is covenantal, the result of a partnership—a marriage—between humanity and God. A covenant (like a marriage) is a mutual obligation that is neither a fact of nature, nor a private and subjective state, but a bond created by a declaration—the word given, the word received, the word honored in loyalty and trust.

The reason that morality is covenantal is that only in and through such a bond do free agents redeem their solitude, creating between them a relationship that honors the freedom and integrity of each while at the same time enabling them to achieve together what neither could achieve alone—the good that exists only in virtue of being shared. A covenant is what turns love into law, and law into love. At the heart of Judaism—its most audacious and least understood idea—is that between heaven and earth, between an infinite power and finite human beings, there can be, and is, such a relationship.

God created nature, symbolized by the palace. But God, seeking relationship, created one being capable of self-consciousness, and therefore freedom, and thus the ability to choose evil. Man, having this ability, uses it. He sets fire to the palace, setting the world aflame. God can, but may not, put out the fire, for if He does so, man is no longer free. A finite being is not free in a world in which an infinite power intervenes to prevent him acting or facing the consequences of his action.

Only man can put out the fire. But man is not alone. For God, the author of self-consciousness, is also the author of language. God not only creates, He communicates. God speaks to man and tells him how to extinguish the flames. Morality is not factual (how things are) or subjective (how I desire them to be) but covenantal, meaning: God gives His word to man, and man gives his word to God. God teaches, man acts, and together they begin the task of *tikkun olam,* "repairing, or mending, the world."[13] They become, in the rabbinic phrase, "partners in the work of creation." Four thousand years later, this is still a revolutionary idea. And still an unfinished task.

The faith of Judaism, beginning with Abraham, reaching its most detailed expression in the covenant of Sinai, envisioned by the prophets and articulated by the sages, is that, by acting in response to the call of God, collectively we can change the world. The flames of injustice, violence and oppression are not inevitable. The victory of the strong over the weak, the many over the few, the manipulative over those who act with integrity, even though they have happened at most times and in most places, are not written into the structure of the universe. They may be natural, but God is above nature, and because God communicates with man, man too can defeat nature. Judaism is the revolutionary moment at which humanity refuses to accept the world that is.

6

The Idea of Man

No NATION HAS DEDICATED itself more thoroughly than have the Jews to the proposition that ideas have power, that human freedom consists of our ability to see the world differently and thus begin to transform it. The natural world consists of causes and effects, events that, given the circumstances, could not be otherwise. The human world is different. It is made in freedom out of choices made possible by ideas. What we think shapes what we do.

Walk into a shop, hand over a coin, and buy a newspaper. No transaction could be simpler. You do it without thinking about it. Yet in this one event you are living on the surface of a series of institutions that, if fully excavated, would tell half the story of mankind. The coin tells of the long evolution of man from hunter-gatherer to city dweller, where specialization and the division of labor led to the necessity of exchange, and thus a medium of exchange, and so eventually money, first as something valuable in itself (precious metal), then as abstract token. The newspaper speaks of a series of technological advances from writing to printing to the most modern forms of instantaneous global communication. It is also part of a political history that gave us the idea that in a free society we are entitled to open access to information.

There are ideas that, once thought, soon become the common heritage of mankind. The wheel, invented in ancient Mesopotamia, allowed people to move objects too heavy to carry. It soon spread elsewhere, because it was simple and solved a practical problem every society faced. Other ideas travel less quickly. They require a specific environment to be able to take root. The Chinese invented many things—printing and gunpowder, for example—long before the West. Yet China did not undergo an industrial revolution. That took place in Europe. Somehow the West had access to a set of ideas, not available in China, that made it possible to create rapid economic growth.

There are also ideas that, though in their most basic form are shared by everyone, remain in their most detailed expression the property of a particular culture. Every society has music, but few develop the idea of a symphony. Every human group tells stories, but only a limited number develop the idea of a novel. Every civilization has a family structure, but this takes different forms—nuclear, extended, monogamous, polygamous—at different times in different places. The texture of family life is often local to a nation and its traditions.

Different cultures represent different lives, different human possibilities that are not available everywhere. It took ancient Greece to formulate the concept of democracy. It took ancient Israel to discover the idea of time as a journey and thus make possible the Western idea of progress. Ideas open doors that would otherwise stay closed to the human imagination. And though they may be taken up by other cultures, often you still have to go back to a particular tradition or faith to find a way of life in its most detailed, richly elaborated expression.

Accordingly, my intention here is to trace the Jewish

journey in an unusual way. Conventionally, such a discussion would center on Jewish history, the story of the four thousand years since Abraham and Sarah; or alternatively, it would describe the laws, rituals and customs of Judaism as a way of life. Instead, I am going to focus on the history of Jewish ideas, the story of how a sequence of utterly revolutionary discoveries precipitated themselves one after the other in the course of Jewish life, each bursting like a firework and momentarily lighting up the night sky.

Milton Himmelfarb said, in words I cited earlier, "[e]very Jew knows how thoroughly ordinary he is, yet time and again we find ourselves caught up in things great and inexplicable." I want to understand why. There *is* something unusual about Jewish life, something found nowhere else, not in the other great monotheisms, nor the religions of the East, nor the secular humanistic traditions that emerged in Europe after the seventeenth century. In the course of my search I am going to observe a simple rule. I am not going to take refuge in the concept of the "inexplicable." We may not succeed, but neither may we cease to try, to understand what can be explained. Whatever else Judaism is, it is not blind faith—perhaps no faith has paid higher tribute to the critical exercise of human intelligence.

• To be a Jew is, on the face of it, to engage in simple things. It involves praying, studying Torah, making a blessing over food, observing the dietary laws, keeping the Sabbath and festivals and striving to maintain integrity in business. It means marrying and having children and holding faithfully to the rules about what it is to be a spouse, a parent, a child. It entails being part of a community, praying in its house of worship, contributing to its welfare needs and playing a part in its collective life, visiting the sick, comforting mourners, participating in the joys and griefs of

others. It means being part of a global people whose home
is Israel but whose communities are spread throughout the
world. These things form the text and texture of Jewish life,
and when we are part of it, they seem as natural as walking
into a shop and buying a newspaper.

But if this is all there is to our understanding of what it is
to be a Jew we will fail altogether to appreciate the ground
on which we stand, the ideas out of which this life is made.
We will think of Judaism as a mere variant on a universal
theme—one religion among many, with its sacred texts, rituals and lifecycle events. Being Jewish will seem to be for
Jews the same as being Christian is for Christians, or being
Zoroastrian for Zoroastrians. In which case, it doesn't matter
much what we are. Presumably all religions are true or false
equally. So why the fuss about maintaining Jewish identity?
If all Jews overnight became Buddhists, they would still be
human beings, still committed to decency, goodness and
the progress of mankind. The world would lose nothing. We
would lose nothing. There would simply be one less faith,
one less language of the imagination. Like dinosaurs, cultures become extinct and yet the world survives and moves
on. But such is not the case.

In Abraham's cry at the palace in flames something happened that would have immense significance for the future
of mankind. In the course of time it would change not only
the history of Abraham and his children, but also the most
basic ideas of Western civilization. As Thomas Cahill puts it:

> The Jews gave us the Outside and the Inside—our
> outlook and our inner life. We can hardly get up in the
> morning or cross the street without being Jewish. We
> dream Jewish dreams and hope Jewish hopes. Most of
> our best words, in fact—*new, adventure, surprise; unique,*

individual, person, vocation; time, history, future; freedom,
progress, spirit; faith, hope, justice—are the gifts of the
Jews.[1]

And though Judaism conferred many of these ideas on its
daughter religions, Christianity and Islam, and through
them to more than half the population of the world, neither
of these other faiths fully adopted the Judaic vision, nor are
they simply the shared heritage of the modern world.

There is a vitally important difference between scientific
and moral truths. A scientific discovery, once checked and
validated, becomes part of the building in which we all live.
Other scientists add new findings on top of it. We don't
have to take it out and rediscover it in every generation. It is
enough that it was once thought and found to work. From
then on it can normally be taken for granted. Moral truths
are not like that. In addition to being thought they must
also be lived. A value, a moral ideal or a social institution
needs to be practiced constantly or it ceases to be. It can be
reclaimed, but only painfully and at great cost. If freedom is
not lived, it is lost, and it takes great efforts to restore it. If a
society lets its family structure disintegrate, it may need little short of a revolution to bring it back again. Judaism is a
set of moral truths—universal truths realized in a particular
way of life. The significance of Judaism to the moral environment of mankind is not just that it thought new truths,
though it did. It is that Jews continue to live them, so that if
Judaism were to cease to exist, something fundamental to
Western civilization would die.

In many respects, Judaism remains a foreign language
even today, not fully understood by others or ourselves.
The whole of Judaism is about the attempt to live out certain ideas about humanity, freedom, responsibility and soci-

ety—ideas of which we, as Jews, may be unaware, just as we can buy a newspaper without knowing the economic, technological and cultural processes that made it possible. But nonetheless we are affected by them, for they move beneath the surface of Jewish life like a vast and powerful ocean swell, lifting us up on its waves and drawing us into its motion.

Jewish life, though it is made up of simple, sometimes repetitive deeds, is the way in which I am connected to a set of revolutionary ideas, monumental in their scope, utterly humane in their effect, which become real in the lives of individuals who make up the Torah scroll of the Jewish people as it has lived its story through the centuries and continents. Perhaps only at rare moments—a Jewish wedding, the Day of Atonement, a visit to Jerusalem, a dramatic event in Israel—am I fully aware of the majesty and mystery of Jewish life. Maybe only occasionally do I sense eternity flowing through my deeds or feel the touch of the wings of the Divine presence. But they are there all the time, and we can hear them if we train ourselves to listen.

We are familiar with the idea that in ancient Israel humanity first discovered God, the one God, creator of heaven and earth. Until then, God—or rather, the gods—had been seen as part of the natural order. Just as there were many stars and planets and countless species of animals, so there were many gods. They fought, struggled, and established hierarchies of dominance, slowly establishing order out of chaos. We have many records of those ancient times, and though the names of the gods change—depending on whether we speak of Mesopotamia, Egypt, Canaan or ancient Greece—

the stories are remarkably similar. The god of the sky does battle with the god of the sea and out of his victory establishes dry land, usually over the dead body of his slain victim. The god of lightning and rain impregnates the goddess of the earth, and thus crops grow and the land brings forth its produce. There is no sharp distinction between nature, the animals, the gods and mankind. Early portrayals of gods, whether as paintings or figurines, often show them as part animal, part human. In the stories told about them they are usually personifications of the forces of nature—the sun, the sea, the wind, the rain. This is the world of myth, humanity's first written attempt to understand itself.

The mythic universe is hierarchical, and what holds it together is power. The ancient world was one in which order was constantly threatened by chaos, at times in the form of floods and droughts, at others by war from invading tribes. Through the stories people told, they explained to themselves why this was so. Disturbances here reflect more ultimate struggles elsewhere, between the gods, the elements, the contending forces that make up reality. In religious rituals people identified with and relived those battles and thus aligned themselves with the victorious powers. If the god of the sky won his battle with the sea, there would be no floods that year. If the god of rain successfully mated with the goddess of the soil, the harvest would be good. If the god of the tribe was strong, invaders would be defeated. If one could only reproduce on earth, in concrete, visible ways, the strange invisible forces that surround us, one could master fear by mapping the unknown.

That, we now know, is the significance of those ancient buildings, the ziggurats, constructed by the Sumerians at the birth of civilization in the Tigris-Euphrates valley and satirized in the Bible as the Tower of Babel. Their architecture was not so much art as cosmology, a theory of the universe given physical shape. The successive tiers of the building represented the rule of the higher powers over the lower. The ziggurat was a symbol of order in which a society reproduced its vision of the world and gave permanence to its own hierarchy of power. The gods were part of nature, and so was mankind. In nature the strong rule the weak, the many dominate the few, the powerful hold sway over the powerless. We don't know whether this was, in fact, the first story mankind told itself about its origins. The most recent evidence suggests that the Hebrew Bible was right to identify, prior to this stage, a primordial monotheism, the world of Adam and Eve, still shared today by the few remaining hunter-gatherer tribes in remote regions.[2] But certainly it was forgotten as people moved to the fertile plains and began the axial stage in human development, the birth of agriculture, the division of labor and the emergence of large, extended societies. As they sought to hold those societies together and do battle with the elements that made life so hazardous, myth was born, the earliest sustained attempt to defeat chaos.

Myth had a particular view of mankind, one that has long held the human imagination captive. Reality is power, and power is the collective. Only when individuals form societies can they defeat the forces around them, and only when the many are subjugated to the few can societies exist. In ancient myth and ritual, kings are, or aspire to be, gods. The rest of humanity, in its various gradations, is replaceable. They are worker ants serving the queen, or beasts of burden serving the master; a labor force, an army; the means to an end. The gradations between ranks and classes were as inevitable as those between animals in the struggle for survival. This was self-evident; it was a law of nature; it was reality.

Against this backdrop a sentence was uttered that heralded the greatest paradigm shift in the story of mankind. "So God made man in His own image; in the image of God He created him; male and female He created them."[3] This single proposition was an explosive charge at the base of the entire structure of the ancient and medieval world. It took millennia for its potential to be realized. But once stated, the rest was inevitable. From it would flow the great ideas that changed the West—the sanctity of human life, the dignity of the individual, human rights, the sovereignty of justice, the rule of law and the idea of a free society. Nothing could have been more counterintuitive. That kings, rulers, emperors, pharaohs were the image of God—that much the ancient world knew. But that we all are—this was revolutionary.

In a study of the moral imagination in Western literature, Lionel Trilling once wrote:

> At a certain point in history, men became individuals. Taken in isolation, the statement is absurd. How was a man different from an individual? A person born before a certain date, a man—had he not eyes? had he not hands, organs, senses, affections, passions? If you pricked him, he bled and if you tickled him, he laughed. But certain things he did not do until he became an individual. He did not have an awareness of what one historian, Georges Gusdorf, calls internal space. He did not, as Delany puts it, imagine himself in more than one role, standing outside or above his own personality; he did not suppose that he might be an object of interest to his fellow man not for the rea-

son that he had achieved something notable or been witness to great events but simply because as an individual he was of consequence.[4]

Trilling is referring to the massive shift in consciousness that took place, sometime between the sixteenth and seventeenth centuries, with the rise of Puritanism. Properly speaking, though, the individual was born long before. It was not until the invention of printing and the spread of the Reformation—during which Luther and his contemporaries persuaded large sections of Europe to go back to the Bible—that the individual was rediscovered and became the basis of a new and freer social order.

The "birth of the modern" was set in motion by two events: the Renaissance, which was the rediscovery of ancient Greece, and the Reformation, which was the reinstitution of certain key ideas of the Hebrew Bible. Western civilization has largely been made up of the interplay between these two decisive and conflicting influences, the Hellenistic and the Hebraic. So fundamental are they, that they are not so much aspects of the past as permanent possibilities in the present. Between them they define two ways of seeing the human condition.

There is a way of summarizing the history of the West in three sentences. In the beginning people believed in many gods. Monotheism came and reduced them to one. Science came and reduced them to none. Or, in other words: Myth was humanity's first attempt at understanding the world. Then came monotheism, which stripped the world of myth. Finally, science taught us that we didn't even need God; all we needed was observation and the ability to connect one thing to another. God became redundant, or at most the initiator of the Big Bang, and the Hebrew Bible was relegated to an early stage on the long road to science.

That is a view we have come to accept, but there is a quite different way of telling the story. From the dawn of civilization to today, mankind has reflected on its place in the universe. Compared to all there is, each of us is infinitesimally small. We are born, we live, we act, we die. At any given moment our deeds are at best a hand waving in the crowd, a ripple in the ocean, a grain of sand on the human beach. The world preceded us by billions of years, and it will endure long after we die. How is our life related to the totality of things? To this, there have always been two answers, fundamentally opposed.

There have been cultures—ancient Greece is the supreme example—that saw the world in terms of vast impersonal forces. At that time, they were earthquakes, floods, famines, droughts, together with the processes of nature: birth, growth, decline and death. Today, we are more likely to identify them with the global economy, international politics, the environment and the information superhighway. What they have in common is that they are impersonal. They are indifferent to us, just as a tidal wave is indifferent to what it sweeps away. Global warming doesn't choose its victims. Economic recession doesn't stop to ask who suffers. Genetic mutation happens without anyone deciding to whom.

Seen in this perspective, the forces that govern the world are essentially blind. They are not addressed to us. We may stand in their path, or we may step out of the way. But they are unmoved by our existence. They don't relate to us as persons. In such a world, hubris is punished by nemesis. Human hope is a prelude to tragedy. The best we can aspire to is a combination of hedonism and stoicism—to seize what pleasure comes our way and make ourselves heroically indifferent to our fate. This is a coherent vision, but a bleak one.

A different vision was born in ancient Israel, one that saw in the cosmos the face of the personal: God, who brought the universe into being as parents conceive a child, acting not blindly, but out of love. We are not insignificant, nor are we alone. We are here because someone willed us into being, who wanted us to be, who knows our innermost thoughts, who values us in our uniqueness, whose breath we breathe and in whose arms we rest; someone in and through whom we are connected to all that is.

There is a line of intellectual development that runs from myth to philosophy to science. It searches for and finds ultimate reality in the great forces of nature—cosmology, astro- and particle physics, neurophysiology, the genetic stream— and the parallel forces operating on society—class conflicts, power struggles, the alternating dominance of successive elites. These are what make us what we are.

The Hebrew Bible represents a radical alternative, one that locates the key to the interpretation of human life somewhere else altogether, not in distant galaxies or macrocosmic forces, but in the human mind. Not in consciousness as such, which we share with other animals, but in *self*-consciousness, which comes from the human gift of language. Because we can speak, we can conceptualize, think and envisage a world different to the one in which we currently exist. This is a fateful power and one that defines the uniqueness of the human situation. We can do more than react to stimuli; we can contemplate alternatives and choose between them. We can imagine and act on the basis of our imagination. Because of this, we have freedom in a way no other life form has.

For everything else, we can give a scientific explanation.

Events are the effects of causes. Determinism reigns. But human consciousness is not caused by something in the past. It is oriented toward the future—a future that is radically indeterminate because it is made by our choices, which themselves emerge from the creativity of the mind. Nothing can predict the constructs of the human imagination, and because of this we are capable of creating new possibilities of action. It is this link between language, imagination, the ability to contemplate alternative futures and the freedom to choose between them that frames the mystery of the human person. It is here that monotheism found God. Jewish faith is the supreme expression of reality as it responds to and affirms the personal.

The account of creation in the first chapter of Genesis is stunningly original, quite unlike any other in antiquity. As the great sociologist Max Weber noted,[5] it is the first time any group of human beings described the world without recourse to myth. There are no contending forces, no battles of the gods, no capricious spirits. God speaks, and the universe comes into being. God is not in nature but above it, transcending it and ordering it according to His word. Nature has no will, or set of wills of its own. It is no longer mysterious. It has become, in Weber's word, "disenchanted," meaning demystified, secularized. This was an immense intellectual leap. It made possible for the first time the concept of science. If God created the world, then it is, in principle, intelligible. The mists of irrationality have been dispelled.

What is remarkable is that the Jewish people did not go on to become the world's first scientists. Instead the Hebrew Bible disposes of creation in a mere thirty-four verses and rarely refers to it again. Thereafter it turns its attention to humanity and to the long, hard journey to a gracious social order, one that honors the "image of God" in mankind. More than the Bible is interested in the home God made for man, it is concerned with the home man makes for God. Fundamental to it is not the natural world God created but the social world we create. That is the significance of the book we call Genesis. Without a certain view of God, we could never have arrived at the idea of a human person. Until God was seen as radically distinct from nature, we could not have conceived of mankind as capable of transforming nature. Until someone had grasped the idea of the Divine creative will, it was impossible to formulate a concept of the human creative will. Theological revolution led to social revolution. In Divine freedom, our ancestors found the mandate for human freedom. In the personality of God they discovered the ultimate affirmation of the personhood of mankind.

That is the significance of the figures of the Bible—Abraham and Sarah, Moses and Joshua, Deborah and Hannah, and all the other vivid characters who make up the story of the book of books. They are the first recognizable individuals in literature, not demigods or mythic heroes in epic situations, but ordinary persons wrestling with moral dilemmas, dreaming of children and a home. In his famous essay, "Odysseus' Scar,"[6] Erich Auerbach points out how much more concrete and human are the characters of the Bible when compared with those of Homer. That is why the histories of the Bible remain so fresh millennia after they were first recorded. They belong to the moment at which man first discovered the individual.

This had huge implications for the way in which it was now possible to think about the human situation. Judaism was the first religion to reject idolatry, insisting instead that only one thing in creation is worthy of being considered as an image of the transcendent God, namely man himself, the living, speaking, choosing, acting, morally responsible person. Even at the opening of Genesis an idea is already taking shape that will eventually become Judaism's most controversial proposition: that since mankind in its diversity cannot be reduced to a single image, so God cannot be reduced to a single faith or language. God exists in difference and thus chooses as His witness a people dedicated to difference.

In terms of ethics, Judaism was the first religion to insist upon the dignity of the person and the sanctity of human life. For the first time, the individual could no longer be sacrificed for the group. Murder became not just a crime against man but a sin against God. "Whoever sheds the blood of man, by man shall his blood be shed, for in the image of God has God made man."[7] Already prefigured here is the phrase in the American Declaration of Independence that speaks of all human beings as "endowed by their Creator with certain unalienable rights." We cannot give up what is not ours. The sanctity of life is written into the structure of the universe by the terms of creation. It is a nonnegotiable standard by which all human conduct is to be judged.

But for the Bible itself the most important consequence was social and political. Even today it is hard to grasp the fact that the religion of Israel is defined as a *rejection* of the two greatest empires of the ancient world, Mesopotamia and Egypt. The two great Jewish journeys, Abraham's from Mesopotamia and the Israelites' from Egypt, are journeys of liberation from existing social structures. Both civilizations were marked by immense building projects, which even today seem remarkable technical achievements. But the Bible sees them not as impressive but oppressive. They were possible only in social orders in which the bulk of the population was, in effect, enslaved. The idea that God is not on the side of power but of the powerless, that the creator of the universe liberates slaves, was the most powerful revolutionary force ever introduced into the political arena. It still is.

One idea—that God bestows His image not only on rulers and emperors but on all men and women as such—had and still has the power to relativize all social structures and thus pave the way for change. In Adam and Eve, the first individuals to be defined not by their place in a social hierarchy but by their relationship to the God who transcends all earthly powers, we can already trace the genesis of liberty. A stunning new vision is about to be born, the idea of a society of free and equal citizens—literally unimaginable before then.

The God heard by Abraham, Moses and the prophets was not a tribal deity, group self-interest projected onto the sky. Nor was He a member of the pantheon of paganism, a capricious spirit invoked to explain why things are as they are, a pseudoscientific construct rendered redundant by proper science. The God our ancestors heard was the voice of reality as it responds to the "I" with an answering "Thou," echoing our consciousness, telling us that we are not alone.

They found God in the mystery and majesty of the personal. Hearing God reaching out to man, they began to understand the significance of human beings reaching out to one another. They began, haltingly at first, to realize that God is not about power but relationship; that religion is not about control but about freedom; that God is found less in nature than in human society, in the structures we make to honor His presence by honoring His image in other human beings. Biblical faith is about the dignity of the personal, and it can never be obsolete.

7

Covenantal Morality

THROUGHOUT THE FIRST CHAPTER of Genesis, the universe unfolds as a majestic set of verses in the song of creation: "And God said, Let there be . . . And there was . . . And God saw that it was good." Then, like an unexpected discord in a Mozart symphony, for the first time we hear the fateful words "*not* good." What, in the divinely ordered scheme of things, could possibly not be good? "It is not good for man to be alone."[1] Yet again we find ourselves at a turning point in the human story. With the birth of the individual, something else makes its first appearance: solitude, and with it, the search for relationship.

This discovery, too, flows directly from monotheism. In the world of myth, the gods were never alone. They conversed, argued, schemed, and fought. The stage of heaven was crowded. Mesopotamia, for example, had twenty-five principal deities. Ancient Egypt and Greece had long cast-lists of the gods. The Hebrew Bible for the first time envisaged a God who was radically alone,[2] and thus allowed man to see himself as radically alone, which is to say, conscious of his solitude. So, within the briefest possible span, the Bible sets out the twin poles of human existence—the dignity of man as the image of God, and the incompleteness of man, the relationship-seeking animal. From this point onward, the entire human story will be about the gradual unfolding of relationships into ever-widening spheres—the nuclear family, the extended family, the tribe, the federation of tribes, the nation, humanity.

The Hebrew Bible represents man's first and most systematic attempt to think reflectively about relationships and the rules and conventions in which they take place. As soon as God is seen as transcendent, nothing on earth—not nature, nor society, nor society's institutions—can be taken as given. Man is at once reduced and exalted. Infinitesimally small, he nonetheless has the freedom to construct relationships and define the contours of human interaction. God is the creator of the natural world, but He has left space for man to become the creator of the social world. "What is man that You are mindful of him? . . . Yet You have made him little lower than the angels."[3]

To introduce us to this new perspective, the Bible uses a device more familiar to us from film than from ancient literature. The first two chapters of Genesis tell the story of creation twice, each time with a different focus. The first chapter uses a wide-angled lens to take in the whole panoply of the universe and man's place within it. In the second, the camera zooms in on man himself, the fissile combination of "dust of the earth" and "breath of God," no longer part of nature but the lonely being only too aware of the gift of self-consciousness that now isolates him from the animals.

To end his solitude, God creates woman. Waking to see her, man utters his first words, and in so doing creates the first poem:

Now, at last,
Bone of my bone,
And flesh of my flesh,
She shall be called woman [ishah],
Because she was taken from man [ish].[4]

The Hebrew text contains a vitally important nuance lost in English translation. Biblical Hebrew contains not one but two words for man. Until now, man has been called *adam*, meaning man-as-biological-species, *Homo sapiens,* that which has been taken from the ground (*adamah*). Only now is he called, and calls himself, *ish,* meaning a person, an individual, a distinctive personality. Here for the first time we encounter a fateful proposition: Man must pronounce the name of woman before he pronounces his own name. He has to recognize the other before he can recognize himself. He has to say "Thou" before he can say "I." Only by recognizing the other as "bone of my bone, flesh of my flesh" do we discover ourselves.

To us the stories of Genesis are familiar. But to the age in which they are set, they are utterly strange. The literature of the ancient world deals with cosmic themes: the wars of the gods, the creation of the universe, the secrets of the storm and the sun. The subjects of Genesis are, for the first time, ordinary human beings in ordinary situations. Its characters are heroes of the everyday. Another fundamental proposition is being formulated: that the moral drama is not about kings and gods but about the here-and-now of personal relationships, the text and texture of everyday life. The book of Exodus will tell the story of the birth of Israel as a nation. By prefacing it with the stories of the patriarchs and matriarchs, the Bible is making a fundamental assertion: that nations are born of individuals, not individuals of nations. The way we order our private lives determines the order we are eventually able to make of society as a whole.

One of the most stunning revolutions Judaism would eventually undertake was the moralization of power, the idea that even rulers are bound by rules. But before that another idea had to take shape—the moralization of sex, the idea that relationships have rules and these are the matrix of morality itself. The stories of Genesis, the prelude to all else, are a set of themes and variations on the family— Adam and Eve, Cain and Abel, Noah and his sons, Abraham and Sarah, Isaac and Rebecca, Jacob and his wives and children.

None of these stories runs smoothly. There are tensions between husbands and wives, parents and children. There is sibling rivalry and fratricide, actual and intended. There is not the slightest attempt to romanticize the family bond. Relationships are difficult, even for these archetypal figures. But they take place in a moral context—the family as the place within which, even if we have to struggle with others and ourselves, we learn what it is to be human.

No sooner have Abraham and Sarah made their appearance than we encounter a recurring and highly significant theme. The book of Genesis describes a series of incidents in which a member of the covenantal family steps outside his or her own territory: the home, the tent, the tribe. Abraham goes to Egypt and immediately fears that Pharaoh, seeing Sarah's beauty, will kill him and take her into the royal harem. The same thing happens to Abraham, and later to Isaac, when they enter the territory of Abimelekh, king of Gerar. When Lot has visitors in Sodom, his tent is besieged by the local populace who say, "Bring them out that we may know them,"[5] an episode which conferred the word "sodomy" on the English language. Dina, taking a walk, is raped and abducted by Shechem. Joseph in Egypt is propositioned and almost seduced by Potiphar's wife.

Outside its own boundaries, ancient Israel encounters a world of sexual anomie in which anything goes. It associates this with other moral failings: murder, abduction, and in the case of Joseph—accused of an act he did not commit—injustice. Two propositions are taking shape. The first is that sexual relationships are the test of all else. Do I respect other people as persons in their own right, or do I see them as means to my ends, instruments of my pleasure? Do I relate to you in freedom and dignity, or do I simply use you? The nature of the sexual encounter will—not immediately, but eventually—affect all other social relationships. Marriage is the moralization of sex, and the breakdown of marriage is the beginning of the disintegration of society, a fact that virtually every civilization has learned too late. The second is that the sign of the covenant will be circumcision, because man needs to be reminded in one place more than others of the binding force of moral obligation.

No sooner has the first man discovered the first woman than a problem arises, in essence *the* problem of all human association. The Bible puts this neatly and bluntly. Woman is *ezer ke-negdo*, standardly translated as "a suitable helper." The translation misses the point. *Ezer* means she is a help. *Ke-negdo* means she is "over and against him."[6] She is not only a help but also a potential adversary. She is a separate self, a person, an equal, not subordinate to the male.

Adam soon discovers that his wife has a will of her own. She eats of the fruit of the tree of knowledge, forbidden to Adam but not directly to her. We know the result. Everyone blames everyone else, and the couple is exiled from Eden. What is rarely noticed is that it is just at this point, as they are leaving the garden, that Adam confers on his wife a proper name. No longer just "the woman," he calls her Eve (*Havah*) because "she is the mother of all life (*hai*)."[7] For the first time he recognizes her as an independent personality. At that point God does a rather moving thing. No longer angry, He makes clothes for them both. Once Adam has recognized Eve as an equal-but-opposite, without whom he cannot beget life, God Himself blesses their union.

Something fundamental is happening here, the answer to the key question of social life. How can there be a stable relationship between two free individuals? How can one person's freedom respect that of another while endowing the bond between them with permanence so that it becomes the basis of trust?[8] To this the Bible gives an answer astonishing in its originality and vast in its implications. Relationships lie not in power but in the bond of mutuality made possible by language. A relationship that depends on dominance—physical, economic or political—is not one between free agents. If I have power over you, my will prevails at the expense of yours. You are a means to my end. This fails the biblical test of treating each person as an image of God. It also fails to redeem solitude, for if I regard you as an extension of me, not a person in your own right, I am still alone.

Words not only allow us to communicate, they enable us to form partnerships. For I can use language not just to describe facts and express feelings, but also to create a moral bond—to promise, to bind, to commit myself. This is what is called a "performative utterance," meaning the use of language to *create* something that did not exist before.[9] So, for example, when I promise to do something, I create an obligation. When, standing under the bridal canopy, I say,

"Behold, you are betrothed to me," I create a new and transformative relationship, the relationship of marriage.

This, no less than the birth of the individual, was a critical moment in the journey of mankind—the still radical idea that the moral relationship is the basis of a free society. The entire complex achievement of civilization depends on groups of individuals working together. I must be able to depend on others, and they on me. But if this is not to be brought about by one of us having power over the other, then it depends on *trust*. And trust depends on my giving my word and keeping it. Just as God creates the natural world with words, so we create the social world with words—sacred words, meaning, words that bind.

This is the first intimation of an idea on which eventually all Jewish history will turn: the idea of a *covenant* (*brit*). A covenant is made when free agents, respecting one another's freedom, bind themselves by a mutual promise to work together, to be loyal to one another, and to achieve together what neither can achieve alone. Keeping such a promise is called "faithfulness," *emunah*, sometimes wrongly translated as "faith." The paradigm of such a relationship is marriage, which brings together in a single institution humanity's most basic drives and concerns—sex, affection, friendship, love, partnership, bringing new life into the world, and caring for it and for one another. Marriage is where morality begins, because it is the supreme example of the bond of trust on which all social relationships depend.

To this day, Judaism is a religion of the family. Marriage, one of the most vulnerable of human institutions, is protected in Jewish life by a whole host of laws, rituals and customs to do with modesty, the separation of the sexes, and the laws of "family purity." The home is the center of many of Judaism's most sacred institutions: the Sabbath, the festivals, the dietary laws, and education as the conversation between the generations.

There is something exceptionally gracious about Jewish family life at its best. On Friday evenings, as the candles are lit, and the blessings made over the wine and bread, as the family sings its song of praise to the mother and parents bless their children, you can almost touch the Divine presence. And there is something moving about the fact that the Divine presence is *here*, in ordinary families in ordinary homes, rather than in the palaces of the great or the cathedrals of the many. Here if anywhere you witness the Jewish truth that God lives in the unadorned heart of the human situation, in the covenantal love between husband and wife on which the republic of faith is built.

The concept of a covenantal bond between God and man is revolutionary and has no parallel in any other system of thought. For the ancients, man was at the mercy of impersonal forces that had to be placated. For Christianity, he is corrupt, tainted by an original sin that only the saving grace of God can remove. In Islam, man is called to absolute submission to God's will. In secular humanism, man is alone in a universe blind to his hopes and deaf to his prayers. Each of these is a coherent vision, and each has its adherents. But only in Judaism do we encounter the proposition that, despite their utter disparity, God and man come together as "partners in the work of creation." I know of no other vision that confers on mankind so great a dignity and responsibility.

The Hebrew Bible uses many metaphors for God. He is a master and we are His servants. He is a king and we are His subjects. He is a parent and we are His children. But for the prophets, the central image is marriage. God is our husband and Israel is His wife. So Hosea put it in the famous passage that Jewish men recite every weekday as they don their phylacteries (*tefillin*):

> *I will betroth you to me for ever,*
> *I will betroth you to me in righteousness and justice,*
> *In love and mercy,*
> *I will betroth you to me with faithfulness*
> *And you shall know the Lord.*[10]

Every other religious value in Judaism flows from this metaphor. *Emunah* means not only "faith" but "faithfulness,"[11] just as in marriage the two partners pledge themselves to be faithful to one another. Idolatry becomes a form of adultery, a betrayal of the marriage between God and His people. Religious knowledge is less a body of truths about the world than a relationship in which God and man come together, as husband and wife, to bring new life into being. The covenant with the patriarchs, and later with the Israelites at Mount Sinai, is a form of marriage in which God says—as a Jewish bridegroom still says to his bride—"Behold, you are consecrated to me . . ." The Torah is no mere document, but the marriage contract between heaven and a people, the terms of their relationship, their bond of trust.

It is hard to do justice to the power of this idea, so unparalleled in other systems of thought. What does it tell us about God and mankind? It suggests that the greatest discovery of the Hebrew Bible was not monotheism, the idea that there is only one God, but the idea that God is personal, that at the core of reality is something that responds to our existence as persons. The assertion of Jewish faith, deeply humane in its implications, is that God is the objective reality of personhood. We are more than mere concatenations of molecules, "selfish genes," specks of dust on the surface of eternity. The universe is not blind to our hopes, our dreams or our ideals. There is objective pain when we commit evil against one another; and when we hope and strive and seek to build, something within us and beyond us takes us by the hand and gives us the strength not to be defeated, to continue the journey despite all the setbacks and false turns.

At the heart of Judaism is a covenant of love. Judaism has often been seen—notoriously by Christianity—as a religion of law and justice rather than of love and compassion. This is quite untrue. To be sure, Judaism is a religion of law and justice between human beings, because only where there is law can there be a just society, and Judaism is nothing if not a religion of society. But between God and man there is a bond of love. No one puts this more beautifully than the prophet Hosea in a masterly pun on the name of the Canaanite god, Baal. Baal was the ancient god of fertility, seen in the storm, the thunder and the rain. But "Baal" also means "lord," "owner," and by extension "husband-as-master" in a world where men ruled over women by force and domination. Hosea contrasts this with the relationship between God and Israel:

> *In that day, declares the Lord,*
> *You will call Me "my husband"* [ishi];
> *You will no longer call Me, "my master"* [baali].[12]

For Hosea, at the core of Baal worship is the primitive idea that God rules the world by force, as husbands rule families in societies where power determines the structure of relationships. Against this, Hosea paints a quite different possibility, of a relationship between marriage partners built on love and mutual loyalty. God is not *Baal*, He-who-rules-by-force, but *Ish*, He-who-relates-in-love, the very word Adam used when he first saw Eve. The God to whom we speak in prayer is not the ultimate power but the ultimate person, the Other in whom I find myself.

This was always a difficult idea, sometimes misunderstood even by the prophets. The Bible tells us this in the story of the prophet Elijah at Mount Carmel. Elijah, in order to defeat the four hundred and fifty prophets of Baal, proposed a trial. Both sides would prepare a sacrifice. The prophets of Baal would call on their god. Elijah would call on his. There would be an experimental test between the two faiths. The true God would be the one that sent fire. The false prophets called on Baal all day, shouting, dancing, working themselves into a frenzy and lacerating themselves, but no fire came. Elijah uttered a simple prayer and fire came. It was a triumphant moment in which Baal worship had been disproved. The faith of Israel had been vindicated through as complete a demonstration as could be wished of the existence of the true God.

However, immediately afterward, Elijah was forced to flee to Mount Horeb, where He witnessed the following vision:

> *The Lord said, "Go out and stand on the mountain in the presence of the Lord, for the Lord is about to pass by."*
> *Then a great and powerful wind tore the mountains apart and shattered the rocks before the Lord.*
> *But the Lord was not in the wind.*
> *After the wind there was an earthquake.*

But the Lord was not in the earthquake.
After the earthquake came a fire.
But the Lord was not in the fire.
After the fire came a still, small voice.
When Elijah heard it, he pulled his cloak over his face and
went out and stood at the mouth of the cave.[13]

God tells Elijah that what makes Him different from Baal is not that Baal is a power and God is a greater power. God is not a power at all. He is not in the wind, the earthquake and the fire. When God reveals Himself, it is not as a force but as a voice, the voice that speaks to man. And not as an ordinary voice, but as a "still, small voice"—the Hebrew literally means "the sound of a slender silence"—meaning, the voice that we can hear only if we listen. God does not impose His presence on humanity. Only if we reach out to Him do we find Him reaching out to us.

It is no accident that the Bible takes marriage as its central metaphor for the relationship between man and God. For Judaism, religious faith is not mysterious. It needs no sacrifice of the mind, no leap into the void. It is precisely like the gesture of commitment I make in a human relationship when I pledge myself to another, whose body I can see but whose consciousness must always be beyond my reach. My capacity to form relationships tells me that though I can never enter someone else's mind, I can reach out beyond the self and, joining my life to an other, create the things that exist only in virtue of being shared: trust, friendship and love. So, though I can never enter the consciousness of God, I can still pledge myself to Him in faithfulness, listening to His voice as it is recorded in the Torah and responding to His affirmation of my personhood. Together we bring into being what neither God-without-man nor man-without-God could create: a society of free persons respecting one another's freedom.

Marriage is the binding relationship with otherness that brings new life into being and allows us to experience the covenantal dimension of the world. Until we can relate to another human being through covenant—the word given and received and honored in faithfulness—we cannot relate to God that way either. The family is the birthplace of our experience of humanity. It is also the matrix of our encounter with God. In truth, the whole of Jewish consciousness is tied to the strength of the family. For without an ordered family we could not envisage an ordered world. Without the trust we learn as children and practice as marriage partners we could not respond to the trustfulness of the universe, which is the experience of reality under the sovereignty of God.

So by now the Judaic vision is beginning to take shape. The concept of covenant will eventually signal to humanity a way of extinguishing the flames that threaten the palace. The covenantal bond is the only way of reconciling freedom with association. It allows us to make marriages, families, communities and eventually societies built on the recognition of our independence and interdependence. It will eventually lead to the greatest of man's attempts to create a social order based on the absolute dignity of the individual as image of God.

And so we arrive at Judaism's most distinctive and controversial proposition: that the particular is more real than the universal. From Abraham onward, the Hebrew Bible begins to tell a story about one family, and eventually one nation, who will become an example to all humanity of what it is to live under the sovereignty of God. "Through you," says God repeatedly to the patriarchs, "shall all the families of the earth be blessed."[14] Judaism is the particular case that exemplifies the universal rule that the world exists under the sovereignty of God, and that every person is the image of God.

I wonder if, even today, we fully grasp what an original proposition this is. Time and again, scholars have drawn attention to the fact that Israel discovered monotheism, and through its daughter religions, Christianity and Islam, taught it to the world. But even monotheism is not as revolutionary as this, the idea of the priority of the particular over the universal, the living example over the general rule. The proof is that no other faith ever adopted it. Christianity and Islam both insisted that theirs was the only true path of worship—that one God is to be served in one way. Judaism is structurally unique—the only world religion ever to believe in a universal God, the God of all peoples, times and places, and at the same time to believe in a particular way of life that not all people have to follow, because just as there is more than one way to be a leader, so there is more than one way to find God. With Abraham something unprecedented emerges into the moral landscape of mankind: a particular family and a singular people whose story will convey a vital truth: that it is in our difference that we are most Divine, and by respecting our differences we do most to bring God into the world.

8

The Chosen People

ONE BELIEF, MORE THAN ANY OTHER (to quote a phrase of Isaiah Berlin's[1]) is responsible for the slaughter of individuals on the altars of the great historical ideals. It is the belief that those who do not share my faith—or my race or my ideology—do not share my humanity. At best they are second-class citizens. At worst they forfeit the sanctity of life itself. They are the unsaved, the unbelievers, the infidel, the unredeemed; they stand outside the circle of salvation. If faith is what makes us human, then those who do not share my faith are less than fully human. From this equation flowed the Crusades, the Inquisitions, the jihads, the pogroms, the blood of human sacrifice through the ages. From it—substituting race for faith—ultimately came the Holocaust.

One people risked its very existence on the proposition that our common humanity exists in and through our differences; that the human person itself, regardless of faith, independent of race, is in the image of God; and that the unity of God expresses itself in the diversity of creation and human culture. With this we come to one of the most controversial of Jewish beliefs, one that has cost the children of Abraham much anguish and suffering: the idea of a chosen people.

What lies behind the idea of a chosen people? The answer is given by the Bible itself in the two stories of the Flood and the Tower of Babel. Imperialism, the desire to place all peoples under a single rule, ends either in a "world filled with violence"[2] (the Flood) or in a civilization that arrogates to itself godlike powers (Babel). Doubtless Israel's historical experience played a large part in this critique of empires.

Most simply, chosenness follows from the sheer logic of the monotheistic idea. If God is the reality of the personal, then God loves the way a person loves, each one separately, for their differences, not their sameness. God is not a Platonist, loving the abstract form of things. Nor is God an imperialist, ruling the world through power and forcing mankind into a single image. God, creator of diversity, loves difference. That is why, though there is One God, there are different ways of finding Him. Every relationship between persons is unique.[3]

The Hebrew Bible speaks of a God who not only loves, but who loves precisely those who are otherwise unloved—the younger rather than the elder; the weak, not the strong; the few, not the many. From this flow all acts of chosenness in the Bible: Abel, not Cain; Abraham, not a nation; Isaac, not Ishmael; Jacob, not Esau; Israel the slaves, rather than Egypt the masters. To be sure, no one is rejected. Divine choice does not mean that God is with this person, not that; with one nation, not another. God—who tells Moses that His name is "I will be where I will be"[4]—cannot be confined to one sector of humanity. That is the point of His remarkable command to the Israelites: "Do not hate an Egyptian. You were strangers in his land."[5] God blesses Ishmael and Esau—they too will become great nations. There is nothing exclusive about the patriarchal covenant: "Through you shall *all* the families of the earth be blessed." But there is nonetheless an insistence on the integrity of diversity, the dignity of difference; the preciousness to God of those whom the world ignores or mistreats. God sets His image on the only creature for whom difference is a source of identity, namely man. And to exemplify this truth, He chooses Israel, the people who are called on to be different, to show that for God, difference matters.

The covenant with Abraham and Israel is a calculated and far-reaching rejection of two other forms of civilization, tribalism and universalism. Tribalism assumes that there is one god for each nation. Universalism contends that there is one god for all humanity and only one way in which He is to be served.[6] Judaism argues that despite the irreducible differences between faiths and cultures, all people are the children of one God. According to the Talmud, when the Egyptians were drowning in the Red Sea, God stopped the angels from singing a song of triumph: "My creatures are drowning, and you wish to sing a song?"[7]

The faith of Israel declares the oneness of God and the plurality of man. This declaration constitutes a protest against tribalism on the one hand, and universal solutions to the human situation on the other. Neither does justice to the human "other," the "stranger," who is not in my image but is nevertheless in God's image. Tribalism denies rights to the outsider. Universalism grants rights if and only if the outsider converts. Tribalism turns the concept of a chosen people into that of a master race. Universalism turns the truth of a single culture into the measure of all humanity. The results are often tragic, and always an affront to human dignity.

It has often been thought that the greatest moral princi-

ple of the Bible is, "You shall love your neighbor as yourself."[8] I used to believe so myself. But I have found that
there is a yet greater principle: "You shall not oppress a
stranger, for you know the heart of the stranger—you your-
selves were strangers in the land of Egypt."[9] Or again:
"When a stranger lives with you in your land, do not ill-treat
him. The stranger who lives with you shall be treated like
the native-born. Love him as yourself, for you were
strangers in the land of Egypt. I am the Lord your God."[10]
In the century of the Holocaust these commands echo with
unrequited force.

It is easy to love our neighbor. It is difficult to love the
stranger. That is why the Torah commands us only once to
love our neighbor, but on thirty-six occasions commands us
to love the stranger.[11] A neighbor is one we love because he
is like us. A stranger is one we are taught to love precisely
because he is *not* like us. That is the Torah's repeated and
most powerful command. I believe it to be the greatest religious truth articulated in the past four thousand years.
Throughout history, Jews were the archetypal strangers.
Abraham says to the Hittites, "I am a stranger and a so-
journer among you."[12] The Israelites were "strangers" in
Egypt. Moses said, on the birth of his first son, "I am a
stranger in a strange land."[13] They were strangers to teach
that God loves the stranger. They were different, yet God
set on them His love, to teach the dignity of difference.

Two ideas have sounded like siren calls through the ages,
leading men to shed the blood of other men. The first is
that God is on the side of the strong, the many, the established power. That is why God chose a people who were
weak, and few, and homeless. The second is that there is
somewhere a truth so universal that it is to be imposed on
all mankind. Behind all religious persecutions is the idea

that it is acceptable to harm other people's bodies to save their souls. In forcing them to accept certain beliefs, the persecutor is acting for their good, serving God through violence to the image of God. Both ideas lend rationale to why God chose a particular people as His own: He chose the powerless to teach that He is not to be found in power, and a people who neither shared the faith of others nor imposed their faith on others to teach that there is not one way to His presence, but many.

Historically, Israel paid a high price for its religious vocation. Time and again Jews became the test case of a civilization. Were they tolerated? Were they protected under law? Were they granted basic civil rights? Refusing to assimilate, insisting on their right to be different, Jews experienced the full force of hatred of the "stranger." Those who persecuted Jews showed that they could not tolerate difference, and a civilization that does not tolerate difference fails a basic moral requirement of humanity. A world that cannot live with strangers is a world not yet redeemed.

What, then, is a redeemed world? The prophet Micah gives the answer:

> *Nation will not take up sword against nation,*
> *Nor will they train for war any more.*
> *Every man will sit under his own vine*
> *And under his own fig tree,*
> *And no one will make them afraid,*
> *For the Lord Almighty has spoken.*
> *For all the peoples walk*
> *Each in the name of its god,*
> *But we will walk in the name of the Lord our God*
> *For ever and ever.*[14]

These words are so familiar today that we need to remind ourselves how radical they were and still are. Every other culture in the ancient world valued victory. Its heroes were military leaders, its ethic was one of conquest and power. The prophets of Israel were the first human beings to conceive of peace, not victory, as an ideal. They were not pacifists, and they recognized the necessity for wars of self-defense. But it remains stunning to discover that God tells David he may not build the Temple because "you have shed much blood."[15] His military prowess, which would have made him the ideal person to build a temple in any other country, is a disqualification here.

The value of peace flows directly from that of difference. For peace in the Judaic sense will come not when all nations are conquered (as in tribalism) or converted (as in universalism) but when, under God's sacred canopy, different nations and faiths make space for one another. No other religion has shared this idea, of a single God with many names, who has set His image on each of us, but with whom we talk, each faith in its own language, each in its own way.

It remains difficult fully to comprehend the vision at the heart of the Hebrew Bible, namely that religious truth is not universal, nor relative, but covenantal. God reaches out to each people, faith and culture, asking it to be true to itself while recognizing that it is not the exclusive possessor of truth. Great harm has always been done to the world by religions when they seek to impose their truth on others by force, or when they treat those who do not share that truth as less than equal citizens.

Today, as Western civilization recoils from the Holocaust, it has moved to the opposite extreme, of declaring that truth is relative and that no way of life is better than any other. This too is false. If moral truth is relative, then so are the sanctity of life, the dignity of the individual, the imperative of peace, the duties we owe future generations as guardians of the planet, and the responsibilities we owe one another as members of the extended family called man. They are not relative. They are the absolute moral preconditions of human life.

Moral truths are absolute but not universal. They are covenantal, meaning, we are called to live them out, not in the same way, but each culture and faith in its own way. God reaches out to us as Jews, asking us to be true to the covenant of Sinai, bringing the Divine presence into the world through the lives we lead, the relationships we form, the homes we build, the communities we create, and the ideals we pass on to those we bring into the world. Ours is not the only way to live, but it is the Jewish way—the particular example that illustrates the general rule that you can be different and yet human, strangers and yet the beloved children of God. I know of no other faith that has taught this principle so clearly, so consistently, so courageously. The Jewish people in its very being constitutes a living protest against a world of hatred, violence and war—the world of the palace in flames.

♦

"When I was young," said Rabbi Israel Salanter, "I wanted to change the world. I tried, but the world did not change. So I concentrated on changing my town, but my town did not change. Then I turned to my family, but my family did not change. Then I realized: first I must change myself."[16] This is the authentic moral voice that has sounded throughout Jewish life since the days of Abraham and Sarah. We can change the world because we can change ourselves. That is the birthplace of hope. We are called on to change the world. That is the imperative of faith. It was and still is a compelling vision.

I have tried to convey to you the continuing power of the Judaic vision, radically different as it is from the conventional idea of faith. It is not a way of understanding or accepting or being reconciled to the world. To the contrary, it is a protest against the world that is, in the name of the world that ought to be. From this refusal-to-accept eventually emerged the most sustained of all man's attempts to create a social order based on individual freedom and collective grace, a society of equal access to dignity and hope.

Judaism is an ongoing moral revolution that began by challenging the great empires of the ancient world. Technologically supreme though they were, they failed the human test. The ziggurats and temples of the ancient world were built by a social order that worshiped the few and enslaved the many. They were neither free nor equal. For Judaism, then and now, the criterion of the good society is not wealth, power or prowess but the simple question: does it respect the individual as image of God?

Judaism is also religious revolution. Alone among the great religions, it argues that there is one God and many faiths—and only one world in which to live together in peace. That means that for Judaism the great spiritual challenge is not so much finding God within oneself as finding God within the other, the stranger. In an age of ethnic wars and religious conflict, that remains a monumental and still-urgent challenge.

To arrive at this unique vision of monotheistic religious pluralism, Judaism had to contain not one religious vision but two. There is the covenant with all humanity through

Noah, and the covenant with one particular family, that of Abraham and Sarah and their descendants. This remains a difficult idea to understand. To give a simple analogy: there are universal features of language, but there is no universal language. All languages contain sentence structures, subjects, predicates, nouns, verbs, markers differentiating statements from questions, and so on. But to be able to speak, we need to possess one particular language—one, not all. And to believe that one language is true, the others false, is absurd. So, too, to believe the idea that one religion is true and the others false is equally absurd.

Not only is Judaism structurally different from the other monotheistic faiths. It is also different from the other great attempt to understand the human condition: philosophy, the invention of ancient Greece. The Greek idea is of truth as system. The Jewish idea is of truth as story. The philosophical quest has at most times been the search for truth that is timeless and universal. For Judaism, this systematically omits the most important features of the human situation, time and perspective. Time is the medium through which we learn, in which we make the long, slow journey from violence to justice, oppression to freedom, hierarchy to equality. Perspective is the dimension through which we discover that there are points of view different from, and not reducible to, our own.

These are not minor differences. They are among the most consequential we know. There were revolutions based on philosophy—the French (on Enlightenment rationalism) and the Russian (on Marxist theory). These began in hope and ended in the suppression of human rights. Nor were the social orders created by nonpluralist monotheisms—the Christian and Islamic empires of the Middle Ages—always better.

Religious minorities suffered persecution, coercion, expulsion and sometimes religiously inspired massacre. They lacked civil equality.

We have no way of knowing what Jews would have done in similar circumstances. The Jewish writer Sholom Asch once thanked God that his people had not been given the opportunity to commit against others the crimes that had been committed against it.[17] Perhaps every nation, once it has power, abuses it. All we can say is this: the conceptual structure of Judaism, with its belief in one God and many faiths, is as near as we have yet come to a world view that does justice to diversity while at the same time acknowledging the universal human condition.

Judaism has a more challenging view of the human individual than any other faith I know. Where Christianity sees man as in need of being saved, and Islam calls on him to submit to the will of God, Judaism advances the daring idea that man and God are partners in the work of creation. Faith is the call to human responsibility.

Nowhere is this set out more strikingly than in the biblical contrast between Noah and Abraham. Noah is "a righteous man, perfect in his generations," a man who "walked with God."[18] Throughout the entire narrative of the Flood, Noah does not say a single word to God. Instead, four times we are told that "Noah did everything just as God commanded him."[19] God instructs, Noah obeys. The Flood comes, life is swept away, and Noah utters no prayer, no word of protest. He accepts the will and word of God. Yet in the closing scene of Noah's life we see him drunk and disheveled, a man who has lost the respect of his children. Noah fails. Noah is the paradigm of religious obedience.

The example of Abraham tells us that obedience is not

enough. When God proposes to punish Sodom and the other cities of the plain, Abraham replies:

> Will You sweep away the righteous with the wicked? What if there are fifty righteous people in the city? Far be it for You to do such a thing—to kill the righteous with the wicked, treating the righteous and the wicked alike. Far be it from You! Shall the Judge of all the earth not do justice?[20]

Unlike Noah, Abraham challenges the Divine decree. This note—the rabbis called it *hutzpah kelapei shemaya*, "audacity towards heaven"[21]—sounds again and again in the history of Jewish spirituality: in Moses, Jeremiah and Job, in early rabbinic *midrash*, the elegies of the Middle Ages, and most recently in the literature of the Holocaust.[22] I know of no counterpart in any other religious culture. Even today the idea that man, "dust of the earth," can debate with God, creator of infinite space, sounds strange and on the brink of blasphemy. Yet it is precisely those who challenge most strongly who are the great exemplars of faith.

To be a Jew is to argue with heaven for the sake of heaven. Jewish faith does not lie in the acceptance of suffering or the escape from it but in seeing it for what it is and contending with it, even if this means contending with God Himself. In this dialogue there are no answers. To expect them is to misunderstand what the conversation is about. If there were answers, we would be reconciled to the world as it is. We would be at peace with a world in which there was sickness, hunger, persecution and violence, for we would be forced to say, "Such is the will of God." The point of the dialogue between earth and heaven is not to receive answers. It is to acquire, through our encounter with God, the strength to carry on, to reengage with life, to build, rescue and heal. In Judaism, God is not in the answer but in the question. There is no answer to the question, "Why do the innocent suffer?" at the level of thought. The only adequate answer is at the level of deed, in the long journey toward a world in which the innocent no longer suffer. To be sure, there is acceptance in Judaism. We call this *tzidduk ha-din*, coming to terms with suffering and loss, saying that "all that God does is for the best."[23] But Jewish law asks us to accept only that which cannot be changed, and there is no evil in the future that cannot be changed.

The significance of this is fundamental. The great literary genre of ancient Greece was tragedy, and tragedy is born in the idea that there is a fate (*moira*) that is inexorable. Man struggles against it and is always doomed to failure. Tragedy in the Greek sense is a concept that simply cannot be translated into biblical Hebrew. Not only is there no such word; there could not be, for in Judaism there is no fate that is inevitable. The very concept of prophecy is the warning of a future that will happen unless—unless there is a change of heart. Israel had prophets; Greece had oracles. The difference between them is that an oracle predicts the future, while a prophet warns against it. If the foretold future comes to pass, the oracle has succeeded, but the prophet has failed. Judaism is therefore the systematic rejection of tragedy in the name of hope.

But does this make a difference now? I think it does—all the difference in the world. We might think that the great Jewish concepts—individual rights, moral freedom, religious pluralism—have been incorporated into the civilization of the West and there is no more work for Judaism to do. I believe the opposite is true. The twentieth century saw a regression from Judaic values, not an advance beyond them.

The whole thrust of modern thought has been toward reducing the sphere of individual moral responsibility. Human behavior is increasingly seen as the product of impersonal forces—economic (Marx), social (Durkheim), or socio-biological (the neo-Darwinians). We are what we are because of things over which we have no control, from the distribution of power to the "selfish gene." Therefore, if we want to change ourselves we first have, through political or technological revolution, to change the world.

Not only is this the polar opposite of the Judaic vision. It is ultimately a despairing vision, because it locates change outside of the individual. It makes us dependent on things beyond our control. A secular ethic will always fail to do justice to the human condition, because it will always see man as part of nature, and nature itself as ultimately impersonal, indifferent to our purposes, blind to our hopes. It will fail fully to understand man as a meaning-seeking, environment-creating animal, driven not by causes but by purposes, shaped not by genetic or social engineering but by free acts of the will.

There are two possible outcomes. The first, which dominated the first half of the twentieth century, turns the Jewish vision upside down. It says that we change the individual by changing the world. The individual becomes subsidiary to the mass, the nation, the state. There have been two such experiments this century—the Third Reich and the Soviet Union. They were also the most brutal tyrannies known to man.

The second, which now dominates the late twentieth

century, gives up on change altogether. Ours is an age of eastern and New Age mysticisms and therapies of various kinds. Mysticism is a way of accepting the world by rising above it. Therapy is a way of accepting myself as I am. Both are ways of reconciling ourselves to a world we believe we cannot change, and both, from a Jewish point of view, are inadequate accounts of what it is to be human. Acceptance of what is, is a failure to hear the call of what ought to be. Judaism has its moments of serenity, such as the Sabbath. But these are mere resting places on the journey; pauses of withdrawal before reengaging with the world.

A secular universe is an impersonal universe, and thus, far from being an advance on monotheism, it in fact puts us back into the world of myth, where man is at the mercy of impersonal forces. To be sure, our view of those forces has changed. In ancient times they were climatic—the sun, the wind, the rain, the storm. Today they are more likely to be economic, political or technological—the globalization of industry, the internationalization of terror, or the erosion of the biosphere. Structurally, though, they are the same. They constitute a view of the universe as a set of forces indifferent to us as individuals, and that none of us, acting alone, can change.

Against this, four thousand years ago, there emerged a different view of human life. It suggested that individuals are not powerless in the face of the impersonal. We can create families, communities, even societies, around the ideals of love, faithfulness and trust. We can change ourselves, and through covenantal relationships with others, we can change the world. Far from being obsolete, this view is as challenging today as it was then. The idols have changed, but they have not ceased to be idols. An idolatrous culture is one that sees reality in terms of impersonal forces. A Jewish culture is one that insists on the ultimate reality of the personal. The abolition of God leads, slowly and imperceptibly, to what C. S. Lewis called the abolition of man.[24]

The first half of our journey has taken us from Abraham's vision of the palace in flames through a series of intellectual discoveries that led to the idea of man, the moral animal, capable of changing the world in the light of freedom, diversity and peace. Necessarily, though, there had to be a second stage. The Judaic vision of social justice could not, even in principle, be achieved by one family alone. The minimum requirement is a society. The Greeks called the basic unit of society a *polis*, a city-state, and from this we derive the word *political*. At this point, therefore, the Judaic vision shifts from the moral to the political, and to that most daring of ideas, a society under the sovereignty of God. At this point Genesis turns into Exodus, the moment at which a family became a nation and covenantal politics—the politics of hope—was born.

Part III

The Vision

9

Exodus and Revelation

IT WAS AND REMAINS the most influential story in the history of politics. When Oliver Cromwell made the first speech of his Parliament after the English civil war, he referred to it. When Thomas Jefferson and Benjamin Franklin were designing the Great Seal of the United States, it was their first choice of an image to epitomize their dream. When black Americans struggled for civil rights, they sang it. When South Americans wrote their liberation theologies, it was the text from which they began. In century after century one narrative more than any other has inspired people to break the chains of the past and build a new society on the foundations of liberty—the story of Moses leading the Israelites to freedom across the wilderness toward the promised land. It is the great, enduring narrative of hope.

By any standards it is a turning point in history. The ancients could understand the victory of power over power. Empires fought one another, armies clashed, and the gods were on the side of the strong. But that God might be on the side of the weak, that He might intervene on behalf of the oppressed, that He might choose as His own people a group of slaves—this was a remarkable turn of events. Individual slaves may have escaped to freedom before, but never an entire population. It was a happening without precedent.

But Moses knew—God had told him—that there was something more important than the event itself. It was to become the cornerstone of a new social order, one never before seen on the stage of civilization. The experience of the Exodus was to shape the entire political vision of the newly liberated people. One day they would find themselves in a land and sovereign state of their own. There would be kings, princes, elites and hierarchies of power. There would be rulers and ruled. In politics, reality rarely answers to the dream. Revolution replaces one set of oppressors with another. The chains are new, the bondage old. That could never be adequate to the religious vision of a free society.

So Moses told the Israelites never to forget. Their laws, institutions and practices would be built around that moment when, as slaves, they first breathed the air of freedom. Time and again in the Hebrew Bible, laws are explained with the words, "because you were slaves in the land of Egypt." Most remarkably and fatefully, every year on the anniversary of the event, we are instructed to relive it. On Passover we tell the story of how our ancestors left Egypt, eating the bread of affliction, tasting the bitter herbs of slavery, and drinking four cups of wine, each a stage on what Nelson Mandela called "The Long Walk to Freedom."[1] As later rabbinic teaching put it, each person, that night, is meant to see himself or herself as if they personally had just been liberated.[2] For the first time in history, memory became a religious obligation.[3] Jews were commanded to become the people who never forget. And they never did.

As we have already seen, Judaism is a religion of questions. The Passover seder begins with the questions asked by a child. Yet there is one question never asked. Why was the Exodus necessary at all? Had God not led the Israelites into Egypt, He would not have had to rescue them and set them free. The story of Abraham and his children might have been quite different. It might have gone like this: Settling in the land of Canaan, Abraham's children grew, prospered and multiplied until eventually they became a tribe, a people, a power, a state. There might have been no exile and no redemption. Why, then, did the Israelites have to leave the land before they could enter it? Why did they first have to be slaves before they could be free?

The Hebrew Bible, the Torah, is an unusual book. It is, as I have said, the unique endeavor to communicate the truths that can never be told as system; the truths that can only be told as story, handed on from parents to children, preserved not as a historical document but as a living memory, one that shapes the lives of successive generations as they continue to walk toward the promised land.

It is the ultimate antimythological story of how God is not in nature, and how man, responding to God, can rise above nature. At the simplest level this means that those who are part of the covenant may never take things for granted. Nothing to Jews is merely natural—not marriage, not childbirth, not social structures, not the possession by a people of its land. Everything that could be seen as the unchanging, inevitable way of things, endorsed by nature or by nature's gods, is perpetually questioned in Judaism. If it is wrong, it must be changed. If it is right, it must be sustained by a conscious moral decision, an act of the free human will.

This is the key to many otherwise perplexing stories of

the Hebrew Bible. Strangest of all is the story of the binding of Isaac. Abraham and Sarah have been promised children. In successive revelations God tells them that they will become a great nation, as many as the dust of the earth, the stars of the sky. Nor will they be one nation alone. Abraham will be the father of many nations. Yet the years pass and they do not have a child. The first recorded words of Abraham to God are, "O Sovereign Lord, what can You give me since I remain childless?"[4] The first Jew feared he would be the last. The eternal people almost dies out in its first generation.

In desperation Sarah gives Abraham her handmaid Hagar as wife, an established custom in patriarchal times. Hagar has a child, Ishmael. Now at last Abraham has a son. Yet God tells him that Ishmael is not the one. He too will be blessed and will become a great nation. But he is not the child of the covenant. God repeats the promise that Sarah will have a child. She laughs. She is past childbearing age. Physiologically it is impossible. Yet the child is born. He is called Isaac, meaning the "laughter" that turned from incredulity to rejoicing. And then, just as the story seems to have reached its happy end, we hear the words spoken by God to Abraham: "Take your son, your only son, Isaac, whom you love, and go to Moriah and sacrifice him there as a burnt offering."[5]

It is one of the most devastating moments in all literature. All of Abraham and Sarah's hopes are about to be destroyed at the command of the very God who had promised them a child. Silently Abraham takes his son, travels to the mountain, builds an altar, binds his son, takes the knife and lifts his hand. At that moment a voice from heaven cries, Stop. "Do not lay a hand on the boy."[6] And so the trial ends, as incomprehensibly as it began. Why the drawn-out hopes, the repeated disappointments, and the final joy only to be so nearly shattered for all time?

The answer is this. What we have, we eventually take for granted. Only what we lose and are given back again do we not take for granted, but consciously cherish and constantly protect. This sequence of events, told time and again in different contexts, is one of the axes of Jewish spirituality. Nothing is more natural than procreation. The entire structure of plant and animal, as well as human, life is directed to it. Every species devises ways of replicating itself and handing on its genetic endowment to the future. This is nature's most fundamental mechanism. But to be a Jew is to see nothing as merely natural, not even the process of bringing a new generation into the world.

Abraham and Sarah had a child because they so nearly did not have a child. Never again, after their experiences, could they or their descendants take children for granted. The years of waiting, the disappointment of Ishmael, the near-loss of Isaac, burned into Jewish consciousness the knowledge that generational continuity does not simply happen. Judaism became, and still is, that rarest of phenomena, a child-centered faith.

Just as Abraham and Sarah lost and were given back their child, so the Israelites in Egypt lost and were given back their freedom. The oldest and most tragic phenomenon in history is that empires which flourish eventually decline. Freedom becomes license, license becomes chaos, chaos becomes the search for order, and the search for order becomes a new tyranny imposing its will by the use of force. That has been the trajectory of virtually every civilization known to man.[7] It begins by taking freedom lightly, assuming that once gained it will continue of its own accord, forgetting that it exists and is sustained only by constant vigilance and repeated acts of self-restraint.

The Jewish people were, from the outset, called on to live out the truth that the free God desires the free worship of free human beings, and that therefore it must construct a society whose members never take freedom for granted. Before they could taste freedom—not merely live it but taste it with the starburst of flavor that only a starving man knows when he tastes food—they had first to lose it. The experience of slavery became, for an entire people, the matrix of the passion for freedom. It became part of their memory, renewed each year and handed on to their children, as the taste of unleavened bread and bitter herbs.

Freedom cannot simply be conceived in the mind and then translated into life, nor is it arrived at instantaneously through revolutionary moments as if slaves could break their chains and become overnight a nation of free people. As the old Jewish saying has it: It took one day to take the Israelites out of Egypt. It took forty years to take Egypt out of the Israelites. Freedom is the political transformation that occurs only through personal transformation. Judaism is the truth that can only be told as story, the truth that unfolds in the course of history, as part of the experience of a people who undertake a long journey, extended over many generations and continued by the act of passing on their memories and hopes to their children so that they never forget where they came from and where they are going to. Freedom is one such truth, and in the life of society it is the most fundamental. When Moses led his people out of Egypt, he did more than remove their chains. He taught them and us what it is to stay free: Never take freedom for granted.

• • •

The Exodus is normally seen as the birth of Israel as a nation. But was it? To this the Bible gives two conflicting answers. The first occurs in a passage we read on Passover at the seder table:

A wandering Aramean was my father,
And he went down to Egypt
And sojourned there, few in number;
And there he became a nation [vayehi sham le-goi] . . .[8]

The other occurs in the wilderness of Sinai immediately prior to the revelation of the Ten Commandments and Israel's acceptance of the covenant with God:

You have seen what I did to Egypt
And how I carried you with eagles' wings
And brought you to Myself.
Now if You obey Me fully
And keep My covenant,
Then out of all the nations
You will be My treasured possession,
For all the earth is Mine.
You will be for Me a kingdom of priests
And a holy nation [goi kadosh] . . .[9]

There is an evident contradiction between these two passages. The first says that the Israelites became a nation in Egypt. The second says that they became a nation only after they left Egypt and had begun their journey through the desert. There at Mount Sinai God offered them the covenant, they accepted, and only then did they become a nation. How do we to reconcile these two accounts?

The answer is that there are two ways in which individuals coalesce into a group with its own distinctive identity.[10] The first is the way of history. Individuals feel bound to one another because they share the same ancestry, the same ethnic origins, the sense of a shared past. When they look back they find ties of collective memory. They are what they are because of where they came from and what has happened to them. This is the unifying bond of peoples and ethnic groups. They are a community of fate, an *am*, a people. The second is based on the future. Individuals can be bound together as a group not just because of where they came from but where they are going to; not just because of what happened to them but because of what they are called on to achieve. They share ideals, a common vision. They participate in a collective life with a distinctive set of rules, values and virtues. They are linked not by history but by destiny—by the journey that lies ahead and the task they have undertaken to fulfill. Such a group is not a community of fate but a community of faith. The Bible calls this an *edah*, a word that political scientist Daniel Elazar translates as "the assembly of all the people constituted as a body politic."[11]

At the opening of the book of Exodus, as a new pharaoh takes power and announces the enslavement of the Israelites, we hear for the first time the word *am* used in connection with Abraham's children: "Behold, the people of the children of Israel [*am bnei Yisrael*] have become too numerous for us."[12] It was then that the Israelites became a community of fate. They faced a common enemy in the form of an enslaving and tyrannical power. Their shared suffering forged them into a distinctive group. To the Egyptians, the Israelites were *Ivrim*, Hebrews, meaning nomads, aliens, outsiders. They belonged to a caste regarded by the Egyptians as unclean. The Torah notes that when Joseph provided a meal for his brothers, they had to sit by themselves "because Egyptians could not eat with Hebrews, for that is detestable to Egyptians."[13] They acquired a common identity through the experience of being like one another and different from those around them. They had the same ancestry and origins. Now, transported into an alien environment, they shared the same fate. That was the first way in which they became a nation.

However—and this is crucial to an understanding of biblical politics—the Exodus was only the prelude to Israel's birth as a nation. The decisive event took place not in Egypt nor even when they left, but seven weeks later as they stood at the foot of Mount Sinai. It was there that they heard the voice of God and received the Ten Commandments, the most famous of all moral codes.

For Judaism, this was the supreme moment of revelation, and it remains unique in the religious literature of mankind. Christianity and Islam are also religions of revelation, but in neither does God reveal Himself to an entire nation. In one He appears to the "son of God," in the other to his "prophet." In neither does revelation have the public character of Sinai, an experience shared by men and women, young and old, righteous and ordinary alike. The difference between revelation to a holy individual and to a nation as a whole is fundamental and defines the unique character of the Jewish project. The revelation at Mount Sinai was a religious moment, but it was also a political event. It is not too much to say that it was the most extraordinary of all political events, more dramatic in its implications than the exodus itself. At Sinai God made a pact with a people, thus creating covenantal politics.

Covenants or suzerainty treaties were not unknown in the ancient world.[14] They were often made between neighboring kings. Three things, though, were unique about the Sinai covenant. The first is that it was made not between one king and another but with an entire people. Before stating the terms of the covenant, God told Moses to speak to the people and determine whether or not they agreed to become a nation under the sovereignty of God. Only when "*all* the people responded together, 'We will do everything the Lord has said'"[15] did the revelation proceed. This is the first time in history that individuals—ordinary individuals, not an elite—were asked to give their consent to a political order. The theological statement of the first chapter of Genesis, that the individual is fashioned in the image of God, here becomes the founding principle of a society. The first-ever democratic mandate takes place, the idea that there can be no valid rule without the agreement of all those who are affected by it. This itself was a revolution in the concept of human dignity.

Far more remarkable, though, was the second fact, that the covenant was made between a people and God. There is nothing like this before or since in the history of religion. Ancient civilizations, however they conceived the gods, believed them to be all-powerful. The gods might be placated, appeased, even sometimes outwitted, but they did not submit to laws. The idea of a moral-legal covenant between the gods and human beings would have been absurd. Yet that is what God proposed at Mount Sinai, and it had vast implications. It meant that right was sovereign over might, and that there is no legitimate government without the consent of the governed, even when the governor is God Himself. This, far more than Athenian democracy, is the founding moment of the Western political tradition, with its emphasis on limited government and the rights of the individual: no power, even the unlimited power of God, is absolute. Above kings, emperors and democratically elected governments stands the supreme authority of the moral law. This is the first and eternal defense of liberty, not only against the tyranny of tyrants but also against what Alexis de Tocqueville and John Stuart Mill called "the tyranny of the majority."[16]

The third revolution lies in the phrase, "a kingdom of priests and a holy nation." We know not only from the literature of ancient cultures but also from the Bible itself that the idea of priests and holy people is not exclusive to Israel. Every nation had its priestly elite. In the pages of the Bible we meet Melchizedek, king of Salem, a "priest of the Most High God."[17] There were the priests in Egypt whose land Joseph did not nationalize during the seven years of famine.[18] There was Jethro, priest of Midian, who became Moses' father-in-law. What is unprecedented is the idea of a kingdom every one of whose citizens is a priest, and a nation every one of whose members is holy. This is the first and most majestic statement of egalitarian politics. Significantly, while the revelation is taking place, Moses is at the foot of the mountain with the rest of the people. At Sinai, God reveals Himself equally to everyone. At Israel's founding moment, every individual is a party to the covenant and none stands higher than any other. Revelation creates a republic of free and equal citizens under the sovereignty of God.

For the Hebrew Bible, there is a difference between freedom and a free society. Hebrew contains many words for freedom but two have particular significance, *hofesh* and *herut*. *Hofesh* means individual freedom, what Isaiah Berlin called "negative liberty."[19] It is what a slave acquires when he or she goes free. They are no longer subject to someone else's orders. They can do what they like. Freedom in this sense can never be an adequate basis for a free society, for an obvious reason. Sooner or later, my freedom will conflict with yours. If I am free to steal, you are not free to own. If I am free to attack, you are not free to walk without fear. "Freedom for the pike means death to the minnows." A society based on *hofesh*—what today is called a libertarian society—will be one in which the strong will prevail over the weak, the many over the few, the powerful over the powerless. In the Exodus the Israelites acquired their *hofesh*. They were no longer slaves. But they were not yet a free society.

At Sinai they acquired *herut*, their "constitution of liberty" as a nation. It was then that they discovered that *God reveals Himself in the form of laws*. For only the rule of law creates the possibility of a society in which my freedom respects yours. Law—a law that treats everyone equally, rich and poor, native-born and stranger—is the institutional embodiment of collective as opposed to individual freedom. At Sinai, the Israelites were transformed from a community of fate into a community of faith, from an *am* to an *edah*, meaning a body politic under the sovereignty of God, whose written constitution was the Torah. At that moment a fundamental truth was established: that a free society must be a moral society, for without the rule of law, constrained by the overarching imperatives of the right and the good, freedom will eventually degenerate into tyranny, and liberty, painfully won, will be lost.

In Judaism, revelation is political because the Jewish project is not to scale the heavens in search of God but to bring the Divine presence down to earth in the structures of our social life. As political philosopher Michael Walzer puts it:

> What is required of a holy nation is that its members obey divine law, and much of that law is concerned with the rejection of Egyptian bondage. In such a nation, then, no one would oppress a stranger, or deny Sabbath rest to his servants, or withhold the wages of a worker. A kingdom of priests would be a kingdom without a king (God would be king); hence it would be without Pharaohs and taskmasters . . . If no member of the holy nation is an oppressor, then no inhabitant of the holy land will be oppressed.[20]

This is the destination of the Jewish journey—the promised land, the holy city, a society of justice, generosity and peace. And in the transition from exodus to Sinai, from *am* to *edah*, Jewish identity itself is transformed from passive to active, from fate to faith, from a people defined by what happens to it to a people defined by the social order they are called on to create.

10

Covenantal Society

JUDAISM HAS NOT ONE political theory but two. Not only does it have its own theory of the state, possibly the earliest of its kind, but it also has a political theory of society, something quite rare in the history of thought, and to this day a vision unsurpassed in its simplicity and humanity.

The theory of the state is briefly signaled in Deuteronomy and set out in much more detail in the book of Samuel. In Deuteronomy, Moses commands, or possibly permits, the Israelites to appoint a king once they have entered the land.[1] For several generations they did not do so. They were led instead by a series of leaders appointed by circumstance, known as judges. Eventually, in the days of Samuel, they asked for a king. Samuel is distressed, sensing rightly that they no longer had faith in him—he was by then old— or his sons. God speaks to Samuel and delivers an unusually complex message. He tells Samuel not to be upset: "It is not you they have rejected as their king, but Me." Then, despite the fact that the request is seen as a rejection of the rule of God in favor of the rule of man, God tells Samuel to grant the people their wish, with one proviso, that they fully understand what they are committing themselves to: "Warn them solemnly and let them know what the king who will reign over them will do."[2]

Samuel duly issues a warning to the people. The appointment of a king will have a price, he says, and it will be high. He will take their sons and daughters and place them in his service. He will appropriate their property for his own use. "When that day comes you will cry out for relief from the king you have chosen, and the Lord will not answer you in that day."[3] But the people are insistent: they still want a king. Samuel duly anoints Saul, and Israel becomes a monarchy. No longer a confederation of tribes, for the first time it has a unified and central government.

What is going on in this sequence of events? In Samuel's speech we have the earliest expression of an idea, reinvented in the seventeenth and eighteenth centuries by Hobbes and Rousseau, called the social contract. The idea behind it is that without law, or at least a central power capable of enforcing it, social life is at constant risk of anarchy, the state of affairs described in the book of Judges as "everyone doing what is right in his own eyes."[4] Hobbes memorably described life in such an environment as "solitary, poor, nasty, brutish and short."[5] For Hobbes the real danger was that no one could be sure of his or her safety. No single individual is strong enough to be able to protect himself against the concerted attack of others. For the Israelites this does not seem to have been the problem. Their concern was foreign rather than domestic policy. They were less worried about the internal breakdown of order than about their continued vulnerability to attack by warlike neighbors.

In either event, Hobbes argues, everyone has an interest in the existence of a central power, vested in a person or an institution, which can ensure that laws are enforced and battles fought under a unified command. However, this power can be brought into being only if individuals are prepared to hand over certain of their rights of property and liberty. The king must be able to levy taxes and recruit an army, which means that he must be able to take something that otherwise would be mine. The existence of government is never painless. It always involves the transfer of rights and powers from the individual to the state. It also involves a risk that the power thus created will become tyrannical and corrupt. That, in essence, is the equation Samuel sets out. The Israelites nevertheless believed, as Hobbes thought rational individuals always would, that the price and the risk were worth it. Without government, life and liberty would be impossible to defend.

It is clear why this theory, the foundation of modern politics, made its first appearance in the Hebrew Bible. It was then that the key ideas emerged of the sanctity of life, the dignity of the individual, the integrity of private property and the insistence on freedom as the basis of society. For the first time, no power of one person over another—including the power of a king—could be taken as part of the natural order of things. The biblical revolution implies that no human hierarchies are self-justifying. Ideally, a society should be comprised of free citizens, none of whom has control over any other. All power structures, therefore, are necessary evils; none is good in itself. This is the single greatest difference between Greek and Jewish political thought, for the Greeks tended to see the state and political life as good in themselves. It also reminds us that in Judaism the measure of God is the measure of man. When God tells Samuel that, in seeking a king, the Israelites are rejecting Him, He also means that they are opting for something less than full human freedom.

So biblical Judaism has a carefully elaborated theory of the state. Oddly enough, though, this is only its secondary concern. Far more fundamental is its theory of society and its insistence that the state exists to serve society and not vice versa. The state came into existence with the appointment of a king. Israelite society came into being centuries earlier at Mount Sinai. The difference between them is that the state is created by a social contract, but society is created by a social *covenant*.[6]

The logic of the covenant, unlike the social contract of the state, has nothing to do with rights, power and self-interest. Instead it is defined by three key words—*mishpat, tzedek* and *hessed. Mishpat* means, roughly, justice-as-reciprocity. It is the principle of the covenant with Noah: As you do, so shall you be done to. It is the legal equivalent of Hillel's famous saying, "That which is hateful to you, do not do to your neighbor."[7] *Mishpat* is the universal minimum of a just society. Wrong is punished, injury redressed. All persons are equal under the law, and all have access to it.

Tzedek or *tzedakah* is a far more radical idea. The word *tzedakah* is usually translated as "charity," but in fact it means social or distributive justice. In biblical law it involved a whole series of institutions that together constituted the first-ever attempt at a welfare state. The corners of the field, the dropped sheaf, and grapes and olives left from the first picking were to be left for the poor. A tithe was to be given to them in certain years. Every seventh year, debts were canceled, slaves went free, no work was done on the land, and the produce of the fields belonged to everyone. In the fiftieth year, the jubilee, anyone who had been forced through poverty to sell ancestral land was given it back. *Tzedek*, the Bible's welfare legislation, is built on the premise that freedom has an economic dimension. Not only does powerlessness enslave, so too does poverty.[8] So no one is to forfeit his independence or dignity. One may not take a person's means of livelihood as security for a loan or hold on to items of clothing they need, nor may one delay payment to an employee. The vision of *tzedek*—a republic of free and equal citizens—is best expressed by the prophet Micah: "Every man will sit under his own vine and under his own fig-tree and no-one will make them afraid."[9]

One way of understanding *tzedek* is to contrast it with two other political theories: capitalism and socialism. Capitalism aims at equality of opportunity, socialism at equality of outcome. The Judaic vision aims at a society in which there is equal access to dignity and hope. Unlike socialism it believes in the free market, private property and minimum government intervention. Unlike capitalism it believes that the free market, without periodic redistributions, creates inequalities that are ultimately unsustainable because they deprive some individuals of independence and hope. *Tzedek* is built on the idea that there is a distinction between possession and ownership. Judaism—despite its two great communist experiments, the Essenes in second Temple times and the *kibbutz* in modern Israel—affirms the concept of private property, possession, for the reason that John Locke did in the seventeenth century. It is the best defense of the individual against the state. The great prophetic denunciations of Nathan against King David, Elijah against King Ahab, were provoked by kings seizing what belonged to someone else. A society without private property leaves citizens at the mercy of rulers. Capitalism tends to democracy.

Large-scale communism leaves inadequate space for individual rights.[10]

So Jewish law protects possession, but it distinguishes it from ownership. All things ultimately belong to God and therefore what I have, I hold in trust. "The land," says God in Leviticus, "cannot be sold in perpetuity, because the land is Mine—you are strangers and temporary residents with Me."[11] There is no ultimate ownership in Judaism. What I possess belongs to God, and I am merely its legal guardian. Hence Judaism's environmental legislation: We may not needlessly destroy even the things that are ours.[12] Like Adam in Eden, we are placed in the world "to serve and protect" it,[13] handing it on intact or enhanced to the next generation. Hence also *tzedek* legislation: what I give to others in need is not charity but justice, not giving away what is rightfully mine, but rather honoring the conditions under which I hold it in trust.

And finally there is *hessed*, usually translated as "kindness" but in fact meaning covenantal love. *Hessed* is the loyalty I owe to those who are members of my family—and a covenantal society is one in which all citizens form a single extended family, as the children of one God. Much of the Bible's welfare legislation, especially those provisions that concern rescuing someone from servitude, is introduced by such phrases as, "If your brother becomes poor."[14] God Himself uses the language of family in announcing the redemption of the Israelites from Egypt: "My son, My firstborn, Israel."[15] This is the origin of the concept of fraternity invoked in the French Revolution. As a secular concept, though, it has never succeeded because the necessary theological foundation—the brotherhood of man under the parenthood of God—is lacking. *Hessed* represents the idea that a gracious social order can never be constructed on the basis of rights and obligations alone. There are times when we must go "beyond the letter of the law," beyond the requirements of equity and reciprocity. *Hessed* is the personal, unquantifiable, I-Thou dimension of society, the compassion and humanity that can never be formalized as law but instead belong to the quality of relationships, to the idea that the poor, the widow, the orphan and the stranger are my brothers and sisters.

Judaism's theory of the state paved the way for the great works of Hobbes and Locke, the architects of modern constitutional government. But the biblical theory of society was far more original and has never been rivaled, let alone surpassed. States are sustained by the instrumentalities of power: governments, armies, police, courts, and the use of force, actual or potential, to resolve conflict. Societies depend on quite different institutions: families, communities and schools, the things Judaism most cultivated and nurtured.

A covenant is not held in place by power but by an internalized sense of identity, kinship and loyalty. This can never be taken for granted. Hence the centrality in Judaism of education, the festivals, prayer and the reading of the Torah. In education we pass on our ideals from one generation to the next. In festivals we transmit our history and memories. In communal prayer we remind ourselves that what we seek, we seek together. When we read the Torah, our covenantal constitution, we reaffirm our existence as a community under the sovereignty of God. I know of no more majestic vision of what it might be to build a society of justice and compassion.

This, then, is where the Jewish journey leads. It began

with Abraham's cry at the palace in flames—a world of oppression and servitude. Covenantal society is the attempt to put out the flames and to create a society of collective moral beauty and grace, one that honors the image of God in every person and thus becomes a home for the Divine presence.

Why then, why there, and why them? Why did these astonishing and still powerful ideas suddenly appear as if from nowhere among a tribe of nomads wandering in the desert more than three thousand years ago? As W. N. Ewer famously put it: "How odd/Of God/To choose/The Jews." And despite the many ripostes, the question remains. If God, maker of the universe, had all time and all humanity to choose from, why the Jews, and why then?

The answer may lie in their marginal, detached situation. Perhaps the nomadic life of the patriarchs allowed them to see the moral failings of the great empires around them. Perhaps the stark landscape of the Sinai desert, between unyielding earth and remorseless sky, gave the Israelites a unique setting in which to feel the naked encounter between God and man. Perhaps Moses' personal history— brought up as an Egyptian prince, then seeing his people enslaved—gave him unusual qualifications to be a revolutionary leader. Each of these is possible, but I want to hazard a different explanation.

The Mosaic books, Judaism's foundational document, sound a repeated note that is altogether strange. Time and again, when we would expect something quite different, there is a reference to education, the transmission of knowledge, teaching, as the essential institution of the covenant.

When messengers come to tell Abraham and Sarah that they will at last have a child, God adds: "For I have chosen [Abraham] so that he will instruct his children and his household after him to keep the way of the Lord by doing what is right and just."[16] This is the only place in the Bible where we are told why Abraham was chosen—not because he was righteous, which he surely was, but because he would be a teacher.

The same, as we saw earlier, was true of Moses. On the brink of the Exodus, instead of speaking to the Israelites about freedom, he instructed them to educate future generations. The most famous of all prayers based on biblical passages, the *Shema*, returns yet again to the theme: "And you shall teach these things repeatedly to your children, speaking of them when you sit at home or walk on the way, when you lie down and when you rise up."[17] There is an intimation here, too clear to be missed, that education is central to the Divine project of a free society under the sovereignty of God. It is fundamental to our understanding of man as the image of God.

What makes man unique among life forms is that he is a learning animal. Unlike other animals, in whom "learning" takes place unwittingly through genetic variation and natural selection, human beings consciously formulate ideas and pass them on through teaching. Doubtless in the first instance this took place by nonverbal training through imitation, as it still does among the primates. At a later stage, there were stories told around the campfire. Almost certainly, this was the birthplace of myth. Later still, more sophisticated forms of communication allowed education to emerge as a specialized function and exposed teachings themselves to critical reflection. Only at this stage, when words have developed a certain autonomy as the language of the imagination, are human beings first able to detach meaning—and thus God, author of meaning—from nature and the world around them.

Knowledge and its mode of transmission are crucial to our sense of ourselves and our place in the universe. There is a technology of knowledge, and there is also a politics of knowledge, which has to do with its distribution within society. Francis Bacon put the point most famously when he said that "knowledge is power." Like all power, it has been jealously guarded. At almost all times and places there has been a "knowledge elite" that maintains a monopoly on access to information, above all to that most fundamental form of knowledge, literacy. Not until the nineteenth century, when the Industrial Revolution created the need for a skilled and mobile labor force, did universal compulsory education eventually make its appearance in Europe and the United States.

One of the most stunning gestures of Judaism was to overturn the whole idea of a hierarchy of knowledge,[18] for if there are inequalities of learning, they will be replicated through all other social structures, giving some people unwarranted power over others. This is the great insight of the Jewish vision, from which all else followed: A free society must be an educated society, and a society of equal dignity must be one in which education is universal. No other people saw this so clearly or so early or put it into practice with greater consistency. And this offers a clue as to "Why them, why then?"

Writing was invented in Sumeria some six thousand years ago. But the three earliest forms—Sumerian cuneiform, the hieroglyphics of ancient Egypt and the pictographic script of the Cretans—were not systems everyone could learn. With symbols standing for whole words or syllable groups, there were simply too many of them to be mastered by more than a specialized group, priests and officials. The decisive breakthrough came with the invention of the alphabet, the first mode of writing that was in principle teachable to an entire population. The first alphabets in history were the family of scripts known as West Semitic that began to appear in the age of the biblical patriarchs in the region known as Canaan.[19]

Their precise origin remains obscure. They may have been developed by any of a number of peoples in that area, among them Phoenicians, Canaanites and the early Hebrews. The very word "alphabet," from *aleph-bet*, reminds us of its Semitic origins. It was later adopted by the Greeks, who turned *aleph*, *bet* into *alpha*, *beta*, and added letters signifying vowels. It is unlikely that the Israelites invented the alphabet, but they were close in time and place to its birth, and they were certainly the first to grasp its world-changing possibilities.

We know from the experience of late medieval Europe that changes in the way information is stored and transmitted are the most potent transformers of a civilization.[20] The invention of printing in the fifteenth century made possible the Reformation in the sixteenth. All the key ideas of the Reformation had already been formulated two centuries earlier by John Wycliffe in Oxford. But it took the invention of printing and the widespread ownership of Bibles before Martin Luther could appeal successfully to the authority of Scripture against that of the Church. Most scholars attribute the later growth of European individualism and all that flowed from it to that one decisive event.

The invention of the alphabet heralded, for the first time

in history, the possibility of a universally literate people. No development could have been more revolutionary in extending human horizons. The knowledge of God, preserved in texts, would then be accessible to everyone—hence, no elites. In almost every other culture, priesthood meant membership in a literate elite. For example, the word *hieroglyphic* means "priestly script"—the script only priests could read. The word *clerical*, which means both "priestly" and "secretarial," reminds us of the long period in English history in which literacy was the preserve of the Church through its control of schools and universities. Only against this background can we fully understand the significance of the phrase that introduced the Sinai covenant—that Israel would become a "kingdom of priests." It means a society in which everyone can read and write, and thus have access to knowledge, power and dignity on equal terms. A kingdom of priests is a society of universal literacy. The invention of the alphabet made this a possibility.

We do not know in detail how the educational system worked in early biblical times, but the Bible has left us one tantalizing glimpse, and archaeology another. In the eighth chapter of the Book of Judges, Gideon is returning after a successful military campaign. Earlier he had asked the people of Succoth for some bread for his exhausted and hungry troops, but they refused. Now he wants to punish the elders. We read the following: "He caught hold of a young man of Succoth and questioned him, and the young man wrote down for him the names of the seventy-seven officials of Succoth, the elders of the town."[21] Even at that earliest stage of Israel's national history, Gideon takes it for granted that a young man, seized at random, would be able to write.

At Tel Lakhish, in southern Israel, chance has preserved another piece of evidence. There, scratched into the plaster of an ancient staircase, are the first five letters of the Hebrew alphabet, carved in the eighth century B.C.E. by a schoolboy learning how to write—the world's oldest surviving example of alphabetical instruction.[22] Long before anyone else, Israel had created schools, not for an elite but as part of the normal process of initiation into adulthood. As H. G. Wells noted in his *Outline of History*, "The Jewish religion, because it was a literature-sustained religion, led to the first efforts to provide elementary education for all children in the community."[23]

There were many great milestones later in the journey: when the prophets began teaching their message to the people, when Babylonian exile forced Jews to think about the mechanisms of cultural continuity, when Ezra set about his educational reforms, and when, in the days of the second Temple, Simon ben Shetach and Joshua ben Gamla created the world's first universal network of schools. But all the evidence suggests that Israel, from its earliest days, had grasped the connection between the invention of the alphabet, the possibility of universal literacy, and the dignity of the individual, shaping its entire theology.

The word *Torah* means "teaching." God reveals Himself to mankind not in the storm, the wind, the sun, the rain, but in the voice that teaches, the words that instruct. The covenant is contained in a text comprehensible not only to kings and their attendant priests, but to every member of the nation, so that each becomes party to its terms and each must give his or her consent before the covenant is binding. The heroes of Israel—Abraham, Moses, the prophets, scribes and sages—are not kings, emperors or warriors but educators; and not just guardians of esoteric wisdom but teachers of the people, meaning everyone. The central institutions of the Jewish people—the family, the Temple, the Sabbath, festival rituals, and later the synagogue—all became educational in character, contexts of learning.

Above all, the key experience of Judaism, from Mosaic times to today, is studying the Torah. This is more than a spiritual and intellectual activity, though it is both. For us, scholarship, study, regular engagement with Judaism's texts, is a political event of the highest magnitude. Every Jew is an equal citizen of the republic of faith because every Jew has access to its constitutional document, the Torah, and is literate in its provisions. As Josephus was able to write with a sense of wonder nineteen hundred years ago, "Should any one of our nation be asked about our laws, he will repeat them as readily as his own name. The result of our thorough education in our laws from the very dawn of intelligence is that they are, as it were, engraved on our souls."[24] A free society—that precarious balance between the conflicting principles of liberty and order—exists not through the rule of law alone, but through a system of education that allows every individual to internalize the law and thus become its master, not its slave. Liberty is not just a society of laws but a society of lawyers, citizens articulate in their own law, each a guardian of justice. No other society has seen things this way. No other faith has made education its supreme religious experience.

Like the invention of the Hubble space telescope, which allowed mankind to pick up signals from the farthest reaches of space and time, so the invention of the alphabet allowed the development of a form of human consciousness that for the first time was able to hear God as the voice directed to the human person as such, and to the construction of a society based on individual dignity and collective freedom. That was the gift of history to the Jews. But there was one other institution central to the idea of a free society, and this was the gift of the Jews to history. Its name was the Sabbath.

The Sabbath was a totally new institution in human history, and at first no one else could understand it. Jewish tradition has left us a poignant record of one such moment of incomprehension. It is said that when the Torah was translated into Greek for the first time, there was one sentence that had to be deliberately mistranslated. It was the verse, "On the seventh day God completed the work He had made." The Greeks could not understand this. Eventually, to make it intelligible, the line was translated as "On the *sixth* day God completed . . . "[25]

What was it that they could not understand? Every religion had its holy days. But none before had ever had a day whose holiness was expressed in the prohibition of work. Greek and Roman writers ridiculed the Jews because of this. They were, said Seneca, Plutarch and Tacitus, a lazy people who took a day off because they did not like labor. Neither Greeks nor Romans could understand the idea that rest is an achievement, that the Sabbath is Judaism's stillness at the heart of the turning world, and that it was *this* that God created on the seventh day. "After six days," said Judaism's sages, "what did the world lack? It lacked rest. So when the seventh day came, rest came, and the universe was complete."[26]

The Sabbath (in Hebrew, *Shabbat*) is a religious institution, a memorial to creation, the day on which God Himself rested. But it is also and essentially a political institution. Shabbat is the greatest tutorial in liberty ever devised. Passover tells us how the Israelites won their freedom.

Shabbat tells us how they kept it. One day in seven, Jews create a messianic society. It is the day on which everyone, master and slave, employer and employee, even animals, experience unconditional freedom. We neither work nor get others to work, manipulate nor allow ourselves to be manipulated. We may neither buy nor be bought. It is the day on which all hierarchies, all relationships of power are suspended.

Shabbat was, of course, the antithesis of Egypt—the free society as opposed to a society of slaves. Slaves work without rest at the will of their masters. So the first mark of the Israelites' freedom was a day of rest for everyone:

> On it you shall do no work, neither you, nor your son, nor your daughter, nor your manservant or maidservant, nor your ox or donkey or any of your animals, nor the stranger within your gates, so that your manservant and maidservant may rest as you do. Remember that you were slaves in Egypt and the Lord your God brought you out of there with a mighty hand and an outstretched arm. Therefore the Lord your God has commanded you to observe the Sabbath day.[27]

But Shabbat was also a way of enacting, while on the way, the journey's end, the destination. Slavery was not immediately abolished; it existed in most parts of the world until the nineteenth century. Even today there are lesser forms of servitude—insecurity, workaholism, the hundred stresses and anxieties of everyday life. And as Marx never tired of telling us, slaves get used to their chains. So, within time itself, everyone had to experience unconditional freedom so as never to lose the love of liberty, even though as yet it lasts only one day in seven. Jews never lost those two memories:

the taste of affliction on Pesach, the taste of freedom on Shabbat.

Shabbat is also a way of living out another idea, the concept of possession without ownership which is at the heart of Judaism's social and environmental ethic. Every week, for a day, Jews live not as creators but creations. On Shabbat the world belongs to God, not us. We renounce our mastery over nature and the animals. We see the earth as a thing of independent dignity and integrity. We become God's guests, as Judah Halevi put it, recognizing the limits of human striving. But above all else, Shabbat is covenantal time, the working out of Judaism's vision of a society of equal dignity and hope.

Not far from where I live, in northwest London, is Regent's Park.[28] Completed in 1827 and opened to the public in 1838, it is one of John Nash's finest achievements. Stretching across some five hundred acres—originally a hunting ground of King Henry VIII—it is a glorious mixture of lakes, tree-lined avenues, open spaces for games, and flower beds that for half the year are a masterpiece of blazing color. There are coffee shops and restaurants, a zoo and an open-air theater and a magnificent rose garden. There are places for children to play and for people to have picnics or rowboats on the lake or simply stroll and enjoy the view. Around it are the great Nash terraces, originally villas, now luxury apartments, with their Corinthian columns, domed towers and decorated facades. I don't know enough about landscape gardening or domestic architecture to appreciate the finer points of this complex creation, but it is varied and beautiful, and like millions of others, I am glad it's there.

What defines the park and makes it so gracious a part of city life is that it is public space. It is somewhere we can all go—rich and poor, newcomer or resident—on equal terms. It is surrounded by private homes, places that I and most of the others who use the park could never afford. But that regret is tempered by my knowledge that something far more magnificent, the park itself, is ours. A park is a public good, something that exists in virtue of being shared. And public goods, by definition, are things I as an individual cannot buy, or make, or own. I can only participate in them by being part of the "We" that creates the shared arena for the "I."

What the park is in space, Shabbat is in time. Shabbat is not simply a vacation, "free time," time that is mine to dispose of as I wish. It differs from a vacation the way a park differs from a private garden. It is a world that exists only in virtue of it being shared by a community. As political philosopher Michael Walzer puts it, "Sabbath rest is more egalitarian than the vacation because it can't be purchased: it is the one thing that money can't buy. It is enjoined for everyone, enjoyed by everyone."[29] On it, rest is not merely something "in here." It is "out there," as anyone who has experienced a Shabbat in Jerusalem knows. The shops are closed, the streets are quiet, there are no cars on the roads. In the midst of the city you hear the leaves rustle, the birds sing, the sound of children playing, the songs of families around the table. You can feel the Divine presence in the public square. This is peace as the prophets envisaged it at the end of days: utopia in the present. Shabbat is what we possess by not owning—it is public time.

The Sabbath sustains every one of Judaism's great institutions. In the synagogue we reengage with the community, praying their prayers, celebrating their joys, defining ourselves as part of the "We" rather than the "I." Hearing and studying the Torah portion of the week, we travel back to join our ancestors at Sinai, when God spoke and gave us His written text, His marriage contract with the Jewish people.

At home I spend time—sacrosanct, undisturbed—with my family, my wife and children, and know that our marriage is sheltered under God's tabernacle of peace. I once took Britain's leading child-care expert to a Jewish school where, for the first time, she saw young children rehearsing the Sabbath table—five-year-old parents blessing five-year-old children and welcoming five-year-old guests. She, a non-Jew, was enthralled. She asked the children what they liked most about Shabbat. They replied: "It's the time when mum and dad don't have to rush off." She said to me afterwards: "You are giving those children the greatest gift, the gift of a tradition. And it is saving their parents' marriages."

Shabbat is where a restless people rested and renewed itself. In ages of oppression it reminded Jews they were free. For my grandparents and their generation, it meant rest from physical exhaustion. For my contemporaries it means release from psychological fatigue and stress. Judah Halevi once said that on Shabbat the poorest Jew was freer than the greatest king,[30] and he was right. In political terms it was the day on which Jews, often oppressed by the world outside, relinquished their burdens and breathed free air. In human terms it was and is the time when we stop making a living and instead simply live.

The Hassidic master Rabbi Levi Yitzhak of Berditchev was once looking out of his window, watching people rushing across the town square. He leaned out and asked one, "Why are you running?" The man replied, "I'm running to work to make a living." The rabbi replied, "Are you so sure that your livelihood is running away from you and you have to rush to catch it up? Perhaps it's running *towards* you, and all you have to do is stand still and let it catch up with you."[31] Shabbat is the day we stand still and let all our blessings catch up with us.

Shabbat is the holy time of a people that found truth in time. The ancient world had holy places, holy objects, holy people. But the first thing the Bible calls holy is time itself: "God blessed the seventh day and made it holy."[32] So Shabbat became our moment of eternity in the midst of time, our glimpse of a world at peace under the sovereignty of God. Within the cycle of the week it creates a delicate rhythm of action and reflection, making and enjoying, running and standing still. Without that pause, Jews might never have continued the journey. Still today, without Shabbat, we risk making the journey while missing the view. It is Judaism's great messianic institution.

But now I want to move on, from biblical to post-biblical Judaism, from Sinai to the last days of Jerusalem. In the wilderness, Moses had given the Israelites their constitution of liberty, their political vision as a free nation under the sovereignty of God. Much of the rest of the Bible tells the story of how they wrestled with this vision, regressing often, but always reminded by the prophets of what their mission was. Several times they came close to collapse— when the northern kingdom was conquered by the Assyrians and ten of the twelve tribes lost to history, and again when Judah, the southern kingdom, was taken captive by the Babylonians. But the worst moment by far was the destruction of the second Temple by the Romans. This time there were no prophets and little hope. It was precisely then, in its darkest hour, that the Jewish people made some of its greatest spiritual advances. It needed to. This time, the palace really was in flames.

11

Tragedy and Triumph

IT WAS ONE OF the most turbulent periods in history. An ancient order was coming to an end, and almost everyone knew it. With the death of Herod in 4 C.E., Israel came under direct Roman rule. There was unrest throughout the land. Jews and Greeks vied for influence, and conflict often flared into violence. There were Jewish uprisings, brutally suppressed. Throughout Israel there were sects convinced they were living through the end of days. In Qumran, on the shores of the Dead Sea, a group of religious pietists were living in expectation of the final confrontation between the sons of light and the sons of darkness. A whole series of messianic figures emerged, each the harbinger of a new "kingdom of heaven." All were killed.

In the year 66 C.E. the tension erupted. Provoked by persecution, buoyed by messianic hope, Jews rose in rebellion. A heavy contingent of Roman troops under Vespasian and Titus was sent to crush the uprising. It took seven years. In 70 C.E. the Temple was destroyed. Three years later the last remaining outpost of zealots in the mountain fastness of Masada committed suicide rather than allow themselves to be taken captive by the Romans. Some contemporary estimates put the number of Jewish casualties during this period at over a million. It was a devastating blow.

In 132 there was another uprising, this time under Simon Bar Kosiva, known as Bar Kochba and considered by some of the rabbis to be the Messiah. For a while it was a success. For two years Jews regained a fragile independence. The Roman reprisal, when it came, was merciless. The Roman historian Dio estimated that in the course of campaign, 580,000 Jews were killed and 985 Jewish settlements destroyed. Almost an entire generation of Jewish leaders and teachers, sages and scholars, was put to death. Hadrian had Jerusalem leveled, then rebuilt as the Roman city Aelia Capitolina. Jews were forbidden entry on pain of death. It was the end of resistance and the beginning of what would eventually become the longest exile ever suffered by a people. Within a century the center of Jewish life had moved to Babylon.

All the institutions of national Jewish life were now gone. There was no Temple, no sacrificial order, no priests, no kings, no prophets, no land, no independence, and no expectation that they might soon return. With the possible exception of the Holocaust, it was the most traumatic period in Jewish history. A passage in the Talmud records that at the height of the Hadrianic persecutions there were rabbis who taught that "By rights we should issue a decree that Jews should not marry and have children, so that the seed of Abraham comes to an end of its own accord."[1] To many it seemed as if the Jewish journey had reached its close. Where in the despair was there a route to hope?

In the encompassing turmoil one problem was acute for those whose religious imagination was most sensitive. What, in the absence of a Temple and its sacrifices, would now lift the burden of sin and guilt? Judaism is a system of high moral and spiritual demands. And as the book of Ecclesiastes put it, "There is no man on earth so righteous that he does only good and never sins."[2] Without some way of resolving the tension between the ideal of perfection and the all-too-imperfect nature of human conduct, the weight of undischarged guilt would be immense.

The biblical answer lay in the rites of the High Priest on Yom Kippur, the Day of Atonement. Once a year he would confess the sins of Israel, and taking two goats, would sacrifice one and send the other, the "scapegoat," into the wilderness.[3] Already, though, before the destruction of the Temple, the priesthood no longer commanded the respect of significant sections of the population. For several generations it had become enmeshed in politics. The office of High Priest was a pawn in the game of power.

What, if not the Temple, could lift the burden of unatoned guilt? Two men wrestled with this problem. They were not contemporaries, though they both lived in the first century of the Common Era. Their answers were both revolutionary and quite different. Eventually they led to a parting of the ways that would have fateful consequences to the present day.

The first was a young man called Saul of Tarsus, later known as Paul.[4] According to his own account, he was a Jew by birth who had been sent by the community to suppress the activities of the new sect of Christians, Jews who believed that the Messiah had come. On his way to perform his mission he experienced a conversion and became convinced that he had been granted a vision of the Messiah himself. Paul never met him in life; he had been killed some years before. But Paul's writings became the first written documents of Christianity, and led it in a radical new direction.

His *Letter to the Romans* is one of the most remarkable documents of inner struggle ever written. Paul, quite simply, was overwhelmed by guilt. He begins with a problem well known to the Jewish sages: command begets resistance. No sooner are we told not to do something than we feel a strong, sometimes overwhelming urge to do it. The rabbis called this the *yetser hara*, the "evil inclination," and they gave it much thought.[5] They concluded that it was a normal part of human psychology, perhaps even a necessary one. "Were it not for the evil inclination," they said, "no one would build a house, marry, have children or engage in business."[6] The moral life is a struggle, they imply, but it is possible to serve God with both inclinations so that the bad can ultimately be enlisted in the service of the good.

Such an answer did not satisfy Paul. In his writings he testifies to a conflict that has, for him, become unbearable. Time and again, he says, he finds himself wanting to do good but instead doing evil. His sense of sinfulness is overpowering. This leads him to the following argument: The law—that is, the Torah—creates the desire to sin, and sin itself is a kind of death. But sin itself was brought into the world by Adam, who ate from the Tree of Knowledge and was thus condemned to mortality. Since we too are mortal, we bear the traces of that original sin. But if one man brought sin into the world, so one man can eliminate it from the world. God had sent His son into the world for just that reason. His death was a sacrificial offering that cleansed humanity of the burden of guilt. In his death, the Law died, and with it, sin. The "new covenant" speaks to the mind, not the body; the spirit not the flesh; it is about faith, not deeds. By participating in the death of the son of God, man achieves eternal life.

In the writings of Paul we encounter an unusually clear example of what Nietzsche called the "transvaluation of values." Virtually all the principles of Judaism are turned upside down. The Law, known to the book of Proverbs as a tree of life, becomes a symbol of death. Death becomes the gift of life. God is no longer to be found in deeds but in the soul. The law of the flesh has been replaced by the rule of the spirit. The sign of the covenant, circumcision, is no longer to be performed on the body but is to take place in the heart. The ancient covenant is no more, and like a woman whose husband has died, so humanity is free to marry again. The old Israel is replaced by the new. There is no longer a covenant with Abraham's children. The new covenant is made with whoever heeds its call.

By any standards this is a radical vision—certainly for the early Christian community itself, which at that time was still loyal to the basic principles of Judaism and looked on Paul as a dangerous schismatic. For them, the key element of their belief was that the Messiah had come—and by Messiah they meant what Jews understood by the term—namely, a human figure who would usher in a new period of independence in which Jews were under the sovereignty of God alone, citizens of the "kingdom of heaven."

What is significant about Paul is that his thought is anything but messianic in the Jewish sense. For him, the new order is not political but psychological. It has less to do with society and its institutions than with the soul and its emotions. His overwhelming concern is with guilt. Had the great rebellion against Rome not taken place, Paul's teachings might have remained marginal. As it was, the Jewish-Christians took part in the defense of Jerusalem and were eventually killed, leaving Paul's theology virtually uncontested.

The result was of the first importance for the development of Christianity. It meant that over the next few centuries, the Church took over many of Judaism's ideas about atonement-through-sacrifice and transformed them from events in real time and space into mystical processes in another dimension. The son of God came to be seen as a heavenly High Priest, or as the scapegoat. At other times he was seen as an Isaac bound on the altar (there were Jewish traditions at the time that Isaac actually died as a sacrifice and was resurrected after three days). In Pauline theology, atonement remains vicarious, achieved by someone other than the sinner himself. It is brought about by sacrifice, with God cast in the role of Abraham offering up his son. These ideas were violently at odds with Judaism itself, which was and remained a religion of time and space, and which saw faith as bound to the physical life of the individual and society. After Paul the breach with Judaism was inevitable.

Within Judaism itself, however, another vivid personality wrestled with the same problem. Rabbi Akiva was born half a century after Paul, and like him experienced a transformation.[7] Tradition tells us that he had grown up as an illiterate shepherd with a violent dislike of rabbis and their culture. At the insistence of his wife, he undertook a course of study and eventually became prodigiously learned, a leader of Jewish scholarship and one of its most heroic figures. Amid the despair at the destruction of the Temple, his was one of the great voices of hope. In old age he gave his support to the Bar Kochba rebellion and was put to a cruel death by the Romans. He remains a symbol of Jewish martyrdom.

Rabba Akiva's response to the end of the Temple and its

Day of Atonement rites was not one of mourning, but a paradoxical sense of uplift. Tragedy had not defeated hope. Indeed it brought about a spiritual advance. The Temple rites might be lost, but they were never altogether necessary. Far from being separated from God, the sinner was now able to come closer to the Divine presence. His words were these: "Happy are you, O Israel. Before whom are you being cleansed and who cleanses you? Your Father who is in heaven."[8]

He meant this: Now that there was no Temple and no High Priest, atonement need no longer be vicarious. The sinner could obtain forgiveness directly. All he or she needed to do was confess the sin, express remorse and resolve not to repeat it in the future. Atonement was no longer mediated by a third party. It needed no High Priest, no sacrifice and no Temple ritual. It was a direct relationship between the individual and God. This was one of rabbinic Judaism's most magnificent ideas—the concept, long prefigured in the Bible but never explicitly set out as such, of *teshuvah*, the "return" of the sinner to God.[9]

To grasp its originality we need to understand two different but closely related traditions. On the one hand, in biblical times, there was a whole series of atonement rites associated with the priesthood and the Temple. There were sin and guilt offerings brought by individuals, as well as the great service of the High Priest on the Day of Atonement. On the other hand, there was the prophetic idea of repentance, which involved no sacrifice but rather a change of the heart. This is how Micah put it:

> Will the Lord be pleased with thousands of rams, or with ten thousand rivers of oil? . . . He has showed you, O man, what is good. And what does the Lord require

of you? To act justly and to love mercy [*hessed*] and to walk humbly with your God.[10]

Similar sentiments can be found in almost all the prophets. What the idea of *teshuvah* did was to bring together the priestly and prophetic traditions into a single institution. Following the prophets it needed no sacrifice. Following the priests it was done at regular times, especially on the Day of Atonement itself. Its real revolution, though, was to carry through into Jewish life the founding idea of the covenant, for in atonement every Jew became a priest.

The differences between Paul and Rabbi Akiva are numerous and significant. For Paul, man is innately corrupt and under the burden of original sin. For Akiva and the rabbis generally, no one is innately good or evil; what we are depends on the choices we make. For Paul, people achieve atonement through someone else, the son of God who died for our sins. For Akiva, they achieve it by themselves, by relinquishing their sins. For Paul there is still a priesthood and a sacrificial order, albeit in heaven. For Akiva the whole system no longer exists. For Paul the distance between God and man has become an abyss: God is high, man is low, and only one being, God-as-man, can connect them. For Akiva the distance between God and man has been narrowed: every human being, by a mere change of heart and deed, can close the gap between earth and heaven. Paul creates a transcendental hierarchy. Akiva and rabbinic Judaism create an egalitarian spirituality. As Rabbi Akiva reminds us, not one but every Jew is the son (or daughter) of God.[11]

Paul's vision eventually won the allegiance of non-Jews throughout the Roman empire. There was a time when a large part of the empire might have converted to Judaism. The old gods of the Greeks were losing their appeal. Jewish life, with its sharply defined monotheism, strong sense of moral purpose, and richly developed educational and welfare institutions, was a compelling alternative.

At around this time there were many converts to Judaism, more than at any other period in history, among them the kingdom of Adiabene in Mesopotamia. In addition to full converts, there were others, known as "God-fearers," more loosely associated with Judaism, having adopted some but not all of is practices. Josephus, who lived at this time, could write, "There is not one city, Greek or barbarian, nor a single nation where the custom of the seventh day, on which we rest from all work, and the fasts and the lighting of candles, are not observed . . . and as God permeates the universe, so the Law has found its way into the hearts of all men."[12]

In the end, though, the stringency of Jewish law, above all the practice of circumcision, was a barrier against its wider adoption, and it was precisely these elements that Paul removed. By the early fourth century, with the conversion of the Roman emperor Constantine, Christianity was on its way to becoming a world power, something which Judaism never achieved.

But within the inner journey of Judaism itself, something decisive took place with the destruction of the second Temple. Politically a disaster, spiritually it unleashed a set of developments always implicit in the covenant at Sinai but never fully achieved so long as Israel was caught in the arena of power. The irony is that it took the loss of Israel's national independence to bring about the flowering of its religious vision. Now that the Temple lay in ruins, every Jew became a holy person, offering prayer instead of sacrifice, and achieving atonement through repentance. At long last the ideal of Sinai had become a reality. Israel really was "a kingdom of priests."

The following speech, adapted from Sh. Ansky's play *The Dybbuk*, expresses as well as any the vast revolution of rabbinic Judaism and the great irony of Jewish history:

> At a certain hour, on a certain day of the year, the four supreme sanctities met together. On the Day of Atonement, the holiest day of the year, the holiest person, the High Priest, entered the holiest place, the Holy of Holies in Jerusalem, and there pronounced the holiest word, the Divine Name. Now that there is no Temple, wherever a person stands to lift his eyes to heaven becomes a Holy of Holies. Every human being created by God in His own likeness is a High Priest. Each day of a person's life is the Day of Atonement. Every word he speaks from the heart is the name of God.[13]

The covenant of Sinai had both a physical and spiritual dimension. It spoke of a land and a society—the "land flowing with milk and honey" and the society that would become "a kingdom of priests and a holy nation," meaning all Israelites would be priests. The nation as a whole would be holy. In the land of Israel, under the sovereignty of God, there would be a republic of free and equal citizens, held together not by hierarchy or power but by the moral bond of covenant.

It didn't happen. Twice the people settled for less. In the

wilderness they made a golden calf, which led to the priesthood becoming the preserve of Aaron and his sons. Later, in
the land, they asked Samuel for a king, thus creating a secular politics which constantly threatened to displace the politics of Sinai. As God said to Samuel, "It is not you they have
rejected as their king, but Me." Israel, entering the arena of
history and power, found itself caught up in inequality after
all. To be sure, the voice of Sinai was never forgotten. The
prophets constantly evoked it, condemning unjust kings
and corrupt priests in incandescent speeches that have fur-
nished the vocabulary of moral aspiration ever since. There
were rare moments, under kings like Josiah and Hezekiah,
when something like the biblical vision transpired. But the
lapses were all too frequent.

Ideals, repeatedly invoked, do not die. They lie like
seeds in parched earth waiting for the rain. It was precisely
at Israel's bleakest moment that something like the biblical
vision did emerge. Monarchy, priesthood and prophecy
ceased, and were succeeded by truly egalitarian institutions. Prayer took the place of sacrifice. The synagogue replaced the Temple. Repentance substituted for the rites of
the High Priest. Judaism, no longer a religion of land and
state, became a faith built around homes, schools and communities. Jewry, no longer a sovereign nation, became a
global people. From that point onward every Jew in prayer
became a priest, in politics a king, and in study a prophet.
For eighteen hundred years without a state, Jews were what
Sinai had beckoned them to become—a nation linked not
by relationships of power but by a common commitment to
the covenant.

Certain revolutionary moments in Judaism are well
known: when Abraham and Sarah set off on their journey;

when Moses led the Israelites from slavery to freedom; when Amos uttered his cry at the corruption of courts and marketplaces; when Isaiah envisioned a world at peace. By one of the stranger twists of fate these became the spiritual possession not of Jews alone but of much of the western world. Two things happened. The first was the unexpected process through which Christianity entered its own orbit and eventually became a world power. The second was that, despite the efforts of Marcion and others to detach Christianity altogether from its Jewish roots, it proved impossible to make sense of the Christian message without connecting it to the history and sacred books of Israel. So the Hebrew Bible became part of the Christian canon, albeit renamed and reinterpreted as the Old Testament. The Mosaic books, the prophets and the Psalms all became part of the literary heritage of the West, endowing it with many of the most famous texts and concepts of its ethical imagination.

Inevitably, though, seen through Christian eyes, Judaism had run its course and come to an end. The "old" covenant had been supplanted by the new. Jews themselves, so Christians argued, had obstinately refused to see this and were duly punished by the destruction of the second Temple. Within a century a terrible theology was born: that the sufferings of the Jews—the loss of their Temple, independence and land—were a sign of Divine rejection. Their lowly position was held up as living proof of the truth of Christianity.[14]

The tragic consequences were immense. The negative portrayal of Jews and Judaism in the early Christian literature led to centuries of persecutions, crusades, blood libels, expulsions, disputations, inquisitions and pogroms. But it meant something else besides. Insofar as Christians knew of Judaism, they knew only of its existence in pre-Christian times. From then on, so they argued, God had transferred His love, covenant and choice from Judaism to Christianity. Insofar as there were still Jews, they lived, spiritually speaking, in suspended animation, mere ghosts among the living. The result was a failure, among Christians and even sometimes among Jews themselves, to understand that Judaism had not died with the loss of the second Temple. To the contrary, it underwent one of most creative moments in Jewish history, a triumph of renewal in the midst of tragedy that rivals, and in some ways even surpasses, the great achievements of the prophets of exile and return. It is not too much to say that it was the moment at which the great ideals implicit in Judaism from its earliest days finally reached expression. And here we come to one of the great unsolved problems in the history of the Jewish people.

Of all the great religions, Judaism has the strongest conception of the freedom and dignity of the individual, beginning with the principle that the human person as such is the one bearer of the image of God. That idea led Israel from its earliest days to search for institutions that would create stable associations combining independence with interdependence. The model it found was the covenant—the morally binding pact between two parties that respects the freedom and dignity of each while bringing them together in creative partnership. This became the model of all three of Judaism's primary associations: between husband and wife, between fellow citizens, and between humanity and God. The question was and still is: How do you combine covenantal society with the secular politics of a nation state?

Secular politics depends on power, delegated and centralized through the social contract, whose first appearance in history was the anointing of Saul as Israel's first king. Inevitably, though, centralized power conflicts with Judaism's high sense of individual dignity. A nation of strong individuals is not easily governed. That is a theme that sounds time and again through Israel's history. The first recorded words addressed to Moses by a fellow Israelite were, "Who appointed you as ruler and judge over us?"[15] Moses was not yet a leader, but already his leadership was being challenged.

Israel's continuing problem was the political stability of a nation comprised of strong individuals. Time and again this created crisis. After three kings, the nation split in two. Always small, and at the crossroads of great empires, the Jewish people needed to be united to survive. Divided, the north fell to the Assyrians, the south to the Babylonians. Even after the return, the nation remained fissiparous. The war of the Maccabees, which we commemorate in the festival of Hanukkah, was as much a war of Jew against Jew—nationalist against Hellenist—as it was of Jew against Greek. Internecine war broke out again in the years before the great rebellion against Rome and fatally damaged the Jewish effort to form a unified resistance. Josephus, who lived through the last years of the second Temple, paints a vivid picture of the Jews within the besieged city, fighting one another instead of the enemy outside.[16]

The story of Jewry after the fall of Jerusalem presents us with the sharpest possible contrast between tragedy and triumph—the tragic failure to maintain a unified state, the triumphant achievement of covenantal society. The Hebrew Bible, far more than Athenian democracy, is the source of some of the noblest ideas in the Western political tradition:

constitutional government, the rule of law, the moral limits of power, the higher law that mandates civil disobedience, the institution of social criticism, the sovereignty of justice, the welfare state. Yet Israel in biblical times held political sovereignty all too briefly, chiefly because Judaism upheld the ideal of the free individual against the power of the state. Moral strength became political weakness, for it meant that Jews were often better at constructing communities than they were at building a state. There is no more poignant remark in the rabbinic tradition than that of Rabbi Hanina, deputy High Priest in the last days of the second Temple, who said, "Pray for the welfare of the government, for were it not for the fear of it, we would eat one another alive."[17] The government to which he referred was that of the Romans. In effect he was saying: Let us at least be ruled by our enemies, for we are no longer capable of ruling ourselves. That is a tragic remark to be made by a member of a people nurtured for longer than any other on the ideal of freedom.

Yet out of the ruins of Jerusalem came a monumental rebirth. As the early-twentieth-century scholar Rabbi Moshe Avigdor Amiel pointed out,[18] Jewry's weakness as a sovereign nation became its greatest strength in exile. Quite simply, the individual refused to bow to the majority. That may have led to anarchy in Israel, but it led to obstinate faithfulness everywhere else. If in Israel Jews were ungovernable, in the Diaspora they were unconquerable. And it was there that they created some of the greatest institutions known to man.

•   •   •

The book of Psalms has preserved an unforgettable record of the depth of Jewish despair at the time of the destruction of the first Temple: "By the waters of Babylon we sat and wept as we remembered Zion . . . How can we sing the songs of the Lord in a strange land? If I forget you, O Jerusalem, let my right hand forget its skill."[19] It was a devastating moment—the Temple was in ruins, Israel was under foreign rule, and a significant part of the Jewish people was in captivity. There was every possibility that Jewish life would come to an end. When the northern kingdom had been conquered by the Assyrians a century and a half before, its population had simply disappeared, the so-called "lost ten tribes." What was to stop the people of the southern kingdom from doing likewise?

As the question was being asked, an answer was taking shape. Groups of exiles gathered around the prophet Ezekiel, who assured them that they would return. But he did more than that. In an astonishing stroke, he realized that though the Temple no longer stood, its memory remained. On this slender foundation something new could be built: "This is what the sovereign Lord says: Although I sent them far away among the nations and scattered them among the countries, yet I have become to them a small sanctuary [*mikdash me'at*] in the countries where they have gone."[20] This is the first reference we have to one of Judaism's greatest inventions. In Hebrew it became known as the *bet knesset*. In English, following the Greek, it was called the synagogue.

The Jewish historian Professor M. Stern states that "in establishing the synagogue, Judaism created one of the greatest revolutions in the history of religion and society, for the synagogue was an entirely new environment for divine service, of a type unknown elsewhere."[21] It would eventually be adopted by Christianity and Islam in the form of the church and the mosque. The synagogue was neither temple nor shrine. There were no sacrifices or votive offerings. It could be built anywhere. It was a place made holy by the simple fact that people gathered there to worship God. It was the most austere yet intimate of all religious institutions. It was the house of prayer.[22]

In this single development Jews performed one of their most stunning leaps of the imagination. At a stroke they freed Jewish spirituality from its dependence on a land, a country, a state, a holy city and a Temple with its sacrificial rites. As Salo Baron puts it, this was a "truly epochal revolution" through which the community of exiles "completely shifted the emphasis from the place of worship, the sanctuary, to the gathering of worshipers, the congregation, assembled at any time and any place in God's wide world."[23] At the same time, though, they never lost their attachment to Jerusalem, turning toward it in their prayers, constantly invoking its memory and the hope of restoration and return.

The synagogue had the most profound political and spiritual consequences. It turned Jews from a people defined by territory into that rarest of phenomena, a global nation. In effect, the synagogue, wherever it stood, was extraterritorial, much as embassies are today. Whether in Babylon or Bialystock, Romania or Rome, whenever Jews entered the house of prayer they were in Israel, speaking its language, remembering its past, dreaming its future. The synagogue was Jerusalem in exile, a country of the mind, the place where the prayers of a scattered people met and temporarily reunited them across time and space. The *bet knesset* was the home of a homeless nation, the center of its collective life, and when the second Temple was destroyed, it sustained them as a nation through the longest exile any people has ever suffered and survived.

It changed the structure of Jewish spirituality. The exiles had no choice but to offer prayer instead of sacrifice, replacing the service of the Temple with the "service of the heart." No less significantly, the synagogue became a house of study, the first adult educational institute in history. From the beginning it was the place where Torah was read and expounded, laying the groundwork for the educational reforms of Ezra when the exiles returned to Jerusalem. Over the course of time, priestly expositions and prophetic interpretations of Torah turned into the rabbinic *derashah* or homily, ensuring that Jews would never lose their living relationship with the covenant, its vision and way of life. Every week they reengaged with its texts, turning the synagogue into the community's ongoing tutorial in its own teachings and traditions.

The Torah was not merely expounded. It was read, or more precisely, proclaimed. The book of Deuteronomy refers to a seven-yearly convocation of the entire people, men, women and children, to hear the Torah publicly recited by the king. This was a moment of national education, "so that they can listen and learn to fear the Lord your God and follow carefully all the words of this law."[24] But it was also a political-religious event. It renewed the covenant with Israel as a people under the constitution of Torah. The regular reading of the Torah in the synagogue, with its echoes of this national ceremony, was thus a reminder and ratification of the terms on which Jews came together to form communities. As Daniel Elazar notes, individual congregations reproduced in miniature the classic terms of Jewish nationhood. "In effect, every local Jewish community, as a congregation, was considered to be a kind of partnership based upon a common contractual obligation within the framework of the overall Jewish constitution, namely the Torah."[25] By regularly proclaiming the Torah, Jews reaffirmed it as the code of their common life.

As the name *bet knesset*, "house of gathering," implies, the synagogue was also a communal center in the broadest sense, home of Jewry's *tzedek* and *hessed* activities, a courtroom and welfare institution combined. The vast synagogue in Alexandria was divided according to trades, each sitting in separate sections, so that newcomers to the city were able to use it as an employment exchange, easily locating their fellow craftsmen.[26] The synagogue became the place where communal announcements were made, lawsuits were heard, and charitable funds deposited and distributed. The Talmud tells us that in Babylon, houses of worship often contained temporary lodgings where visitors could receive hospitality.[27]

▸ So, by the time crisis again threatened the Jewish people, with the destruction of the second Temple in 70 C.E. and the suppression of the Bar Kochba revolt sixty-five years later, an institution already existed that was to prove capable of one of the most remarkable of all achievements of religious and cultural continuity: the sustaining of Jewish identity through centuries of global dispersion. In the synagogue, Jews were able to keep alive the three things on which their existence depended, *Torah* or Jewish study, *avodah* or Jewish worship, and *gemilut hassadim*, acts of social welfare.[28] It was their school, their miniature Temple and their social center. It became their matrix of belonging, the place in which they reaffirmed the classic terms of Jewish existence and their membership in the great chain of the generations.

Not only did the synagogue represent the moment of the revelation at Sinai when Jews were transformed from an *am* to an *edah*, from a community of fate to one of faith. It also served as a recreation of the *mishkan*, or tabernacle in the wilderness, Israel's first house of collective worship. Unlike the Temple in Jerusalem, the tabernacle had no fixed address. It was erected wherever they made camp, and dismantled and carried when they moved on. It became a symbol of Israel's journey as an ever-moving people, and of the fact that wherever Jews went, the Divine presence went with them. The tabernacle at the center of the camp defined Israel as the people in whose midst is the space we make for God.

As I pointed out earlier, the Torah devotes a mere thirty-four verses to God's creation of the universe. It dedicates some six hundred verses to the Israelites' construction of the tabernacle, a fragile structure of coverings and beams. This implies that although the Torah is interested in the natural universe, the home God makes for man, it is even more interested in the social universe, the home man makes for God. It is said that when the Roman general Pompey entered the Holy of Holies in Jerusalem, he was astonished to find it bare of all icons and sacred objects. Just as the Sabbath is empty time, so the tabernacle was empty space—signaling Judaism's great spiritual axiom, that God lives in the room we make for him in the human heart.

King Solomon, dedicating the first Temple, asked a simple metaphysical question. "But will God really dwell on earth? The heavens, even the highest heavens, cannot contain You. How much less this house that I have built!"[29]

How can an infinite God inhabit finite space? The answer, always implicit in the Hebrew Bible, was given most beautifully by a great Hassidic rabbi, Menahem Mendel of Kotsk. It is said that he once asked his disciples, "Where does God live?" They were bewildered. "How can the rabbi ask, Where does God live? Where does God *not* live?" "No," said the rabbi, "God lives where we let Him in."[30]

The synagogue was one of Jewry's greatest creations. It sustained the Jewish people through almost two thousand years of exile. It kept them together as the only nation ever to survive an extended period without a land, a country or political power, dispersed throughout the world. It was their spiritual home, educational citadel and welfare center, and it connected them to all other Jews through time and space. Wherever ten Jews gathered and formed a community, it was as if they were the entire Jewish people in microcosm. Wherever they prayed was a fragment of Jerusalem. Whenever they sat and studied it was as if they were back at Sinai. In the *bet knesset* the scattered descendants of a once-compact nation gathered and reconstituted themselves as a single people united across boundaries by a shared history and hope. And by building communities around the synagogue in space, and the Sabbath in time, Jews became the living circle at whose center is God.

12

Truth Lived

TRADITION HAS CAUGHT and fixed, as if in amber, one other moment that signaled a great turn in the Jewish journey. Rabban Johanan ben Zakkai, leader of the moderates at the time of the great rebellion, was smuggled out of the besieged Jerusalem in a coffin to conduct negotiations with Vespasian, leader of the Roman army and soon to become emperor. In return for surrender he asked for one thing above all else. "Give me," he is reported to have said, "the academy of Yavneh and its sages."[1] Once again, as at the time of Moses and the Exodus, and again in Babylon in the days of Ezekiel, a crisis in Jewish history was met by an ancient intuition. To defend a country, you need an army. But to defend an identity, you need a school. Judaism was about to become again a religion of the book, not the sword.

From earliest times, the great leaders of Israel predicated the survival of their people and its mission on the most insubstantial thing of all: words, a text, the Torah. The covenant at Sinai did more than turn Israel into "the people of the book." It created a nation whose very identity depended on that book. It was, at one and the same time, their constitution as a nation, their law as a society, their history

as a people, their vocation as a faith, and the physical reminder of this covenant with God. At times they drifted
from it and were summoned back by the prophets and the
more conscientious priests and kings. Now, though, it was
their only hope. And as if in preparation for the hour of
need, for some centuries they had been making it a new
home. The Mosaic books see the family as the great educational institution. The Babylonian exile added the synagogue. The period between the Maccabean uprising and
the fall of Jerusalem saw the emergence of three other intellectual centers: the academy or *yeshivah*, the *bet midrash* or
house of study, and the school. The school was for children,
the *bet midrash* for adult education, and the academy for
higher study, Judaism's own university.

Already before the destruction of the Temple, Jews had
created the world's first system of universal, free, compulsory education. By the first century Joshua ben Gamla had
established a comprehensive network of primary schools
throughout Judea.[2] Beyond school came the weekly adult
encounter with learning in the synagogue, or *bet midrash*.
Beyond that were the great *yeshivot*, such as the Houses of
Hillel and Shammai, or the academy at Yavneh, training
grounds of Judaism's sages—the *hakhamim*, or rabbis, who
for the next two thousand years became its teachers and
leaders, its equivalents of Plato's philosopher-kings. There
was nothing remotely like this educational infrastructure in
the ancient world. Even the great academies of ancient
Greece were confined to an elite. It achieved more than the
creation of a universally literate society. Paul Johnson
rightly describes it as an "ancient and highly efficient social
machine for the production of intellectuals."[3]

The story of the Jewish people, especially after the second Temple, is about one of the great love affairs of all time,

the love of a people for a book, the Torah. Much of the rabbinic literature, especially the tractate *Avot, Ethics of the Fathers*, reads like an extended poem in praise of Torah and
the life of learning. The Torah was, said the rabbis, the architecture of creation, written in letters of black fire on
white fire.[4] It was, said a later mystical tradition, nothing
less than a single extended name of God.[5] For Rabbi Akiva,
it was the very air Jews breathed.[6] It was life itself.

The sages told a fascinating story about King David.
Once, they said, he asked God to tell him when he would
die. God refused to answer, saying only that David's last day
would be a Sabbath. Every Shabbat thereafter, David spent
the whole day in study. When the moment came for him to
die, the angel of death found him engaged in learning, not
pausing for interruption. As long as he studied, says the Talmud, death had no power over him. The angel devised a
stratagem. It made a rustling sound in a nearby tree. Climb-
ing a ladder to see what was making the noise, David
slipped and fell. For a second, no Torah came from his lips,
and at that moment he died.[7] This story tells us what had
changed in the Jewish mind. David, in the rabbinic imagination, had ceased to be a military hero, victor of Israel's
greatest battles, and become instead a sage, and a new kind
of symbol of the Jewish people. So long as it keeps studying, the story implied, the Jewish people cannot die.

To a degree unrivaled by any other nation, Jews became
a people whose very survival was predicated on the school,
the house of study, and life as a never-ending process of
learning. "When does the obligation to study begin?" asks
Maimonides. "As soon as a child can talk. When does it
end? On the day of death."[8] So, throughout the ages, Jewish
communities made education their first priority. Benjamin
of Tudela, traveling in Provence in 1165, could report that

in Posquieres, a town of a mere forty Jews, there was a great *yeshivah*. Marseilles, whose Jewish population numbered three hundred, was "a city of *geonim* [outstanding scholars] and sages."[9]

In fifteenth-century Spain, where Jews were facing constant persecution, the 1432 Valladolid Synod established taxes on meat and wine, circumcisions, weddings and funerals, to create a fund to establish schools in every community where there were fifteen householders.[10] Phenomena like these could be found in virtually every Jewish community throughout the Middle Ages. At a time when their neighbors were often illiterate, Jews lived a life devoted to study and gave the seats of honor by the eastern wall of the synagogue to scholars. A twelfth-century monk, one of Abelard's disciples, wrote that "a Jew, however poor, if he had ten sons, would put them all to letters, and not for gain as the Christians do, but for the understanding of God's law; and not only his sons but his daughters."[11]

The result was a constant dialogue with revelation. In study Jews found themselves entering into a conversation not only with the Torah but with successive generations of its commentators, Hillel and Shammai, Rav and Shmuel, Abaye and Rava, Rashi and the Tosafists, Maimonides and Nahmanides. On virtually every subject they had access to a millennial heritage of wisdom. Landless and powerless, they inhabited a mental universe whose horizons in space and time were vast. And as each community, each age, added its *hiddushim*, its new insights into the ancient text, they could feel some of the excitement of Sinai. Judaism is not a religion of continuing revelation, but rather one of continuing interpretation.

Nor were Jews insensitive to wider currents of thought,

though they were often excluded from them. Judaism's earliest sages drew a careful distinction—exactly paralleling the distinction between the Noahide and Sinai covenants—between *hokhmah* and *Torah*, "wisdom" and revealed truth. Wisdom was the universal property of mankind. Torah was the particular heritage of Israel. Wisdom could be acquired from any source. "Accept the truth," said Maimonides, "whoever says it."[12] Torah was acquired by discipleship, from parents and, above all, teachers. Jews, whether in the Hellenistic age, or more recently in the nineteenth century, were rarely troubled by apparent conflicts between science and religion. They rightly realized that they were separate realms, the worlds of what is and what ought to be. The great rabbis were often people of wide humanistic learning. Maimonides' first book was on logic, and he wrote no less than eight medical textbooks.

The great object of Torah study, though, was the life of faith itself: what became known, appropriately for a people on a journey, as *halakhah*, "the way." Every aspect of life— not just religious ritual but business and commercial transactions, relationships between husband and wife, parents and children, food and sex—had its precisely calibrated laws, its choreography of holiness. The fundamental idea of Judaism was and is that we bring God into the world through daily acts and interactions, precisely as the book of Genesis portrays the religious drama in terms of ordinary lives. The home, the workplace and the marketplace are religious arenas no less than the synagogue. As the late Yeshayahu Leibowitz put it, Judaism is a religion not just of poetry but also of prose.[13] Of course, this had been the message of the prophets. Amos, Hosea, Micah, Isaiah, all saw equity, generosity, justice and civility as the tests of life lived in response to God. But where they failed, the rabbis succeeded. Without the prophets' incandescent rhetoric, they nonetheless succeeded, in tough times, in creating living communities of collective grace. It was as if, having lost the Temple, Jews rebuilt it in place after place with deeds instead of stones, words instead of mortar. The *Shekhinah*, God's indwelling presence, found its home in human lives.

But the achievements of the world of Torah were not only spiritual and moral; they were also political. For it was here, in the arena of Torah study, that the sages fought, and to a considerable degree won, the great battle of covenantal politics, fashioning a society of equal access to human dignity. Recall the axiom of democratic spirituality: Since knowledge is power, and the distribution of power is the central concern of politics, then the distribution of knowledge is the single greatest issue affecting the structure of society. It was not on the streets or behind the barricades but in the house of study that the rabbis achieved the three great ideals later articulated in the French Revolution: equality, liberty and fraternity.

Judaism is an egalitarian faith, but throughout the biblical era Israel remained a hierarchical society. There were kings and priests, dynastic rulers of the temporal and spiritual domains. Only when these disappeared could Israel genuinely become a kingdom, all of whose members were priests. The rabbis' statements on status in a Torah society are blunt. "A bastard scholar takes precedence over an ignorant High Priest."[14] "There are three crowns in Israel. The crown of priesthood went to Aaron and his descendants. The crown of kingship went to David and his successors. But the crown of Torah lies in front of every Jew. Whoever wishes, let him come and take it."[15] These are overtly egalitarian statements, implying that universal education signaled the end of dynastic elites.

Liberty, too, had been a Jewish problem since the Exodus. How do you combine freedom and association, liberty and law? Laws are constraints on freedom unless they coincide with what I desire. But this means that liberty is above all a problem of education. For if law and desire conflict, what I experience is not freedom but constraint. Only if my desires have been educated beyond selfishness to the common good do I experience law as freedom itself—as the Psalm put it: "I will walk in freedom for I have sought out Your law."[16] By a delightful exegetical pun, the rabbis read the description of the tablets brought by Moses from the mountain, not as "the writing was the writing of God, engraved (*harut*) on the tablets," but as "freedom (*herut*) was on the tablets."[17] Meaning, only when education has engraved the law into the hearts of its citizens do we experience collective freedom.

Thus equality and liberty. But how do you create fraternity in a people as fractious as the Jews? The rabbis' answer lay in translating conflict into argument and making argument itself the pulse of intellectual life. The entire rabbinic literature is nothing less than an anthology of what the sages called "argument for the sake of heaven."[18] Having inherited a world in which, through internal conflict, Jews had brought disaster on themselves, the rabbis took disagreement and relocated it within the house of study. There and there alone were Jews able to construct out of a culture of strong individuals and sharply conflicting views, *hevrutah*, the "fellowship" of study.

· · ·

The Jewish vision, complex, subtle, and set out in a vast literature that has been studied for generations, is built on simple ideas. Because God is above nature, we—through our capacity for self-consciousness, imagination and choice—are capable of rising above our nature, brutal and aggressive though it often is. As *Homo sapiens,* biological beings, we are "dust of the earth." But within us also is the breath of God. Marxism, neo-Darwinism and the many other forms of determinism are false to our most basic experience of the moral life. A thousand times a day we choose. We say this rather than that; do one thing rather than another; and we know that had we chosen differently we would have spoken or acted differently. From this simple fact flows the momentous truth: because we can change ourselves, together we can change the world.

But that needs a massive effort of togetherness. It is the work not of individuals but of families and communities throughout the world and of many generations. Much of Judaism is about creating those structures of togetherness in a way that honors individuality and yet brings us together to create the things that exist only by virtue of being shared. Judaism is the ambitious attempt to build a society out of covenantal relationships, associations of free individuals, each respecting the integrity of the other, bound only by words, moral commitments, given, received and honored in trust. The concept of covenant not only shaped the Jewish view of social institutions but also and fundamentally our view of the relationship between humanity and God. Though, early in its history, Israel saw God as intervening in the affairs of man—in the Flood, the Exodus, the wilderness, the conquest of the land—that was only in the childhood of the world. God is the call to human responsibility, the voice that we hear only if we first learn how to listen, the voice that summons us to act.

How, then, do these ideas connect with Jewish life? It is helpful in this context to contrast Judaism, as the life of faith, with the civilization of ancient Greece and its supreme expression, namely philosophy. Philosophy represents truth thought, whereas Judaism represents truth lived. Greece is the paradigm of *hokhmah*, the search for knowledge of what is. Judaism is the religion of *Torah*, which is to say covenantal knowledge of what ought to be. So, though Judaism is a set of beliefs, it is not a creed in the conventional sense. Instead, it is a series of truths that become true only in virtue of the fact that we have lived them. In living them, we turn the "ought" into the "is." We make a fragment of perfection in an imperfect world and create a living truth, a life of faith. By keeping *mitzvot*, following the commandments—or more precisely, bringing God, the voice of the world that ought to be, into the world that is— we bring heaven down to earth.

Most of the commandments fall into one of three categories. There are those loosely called *mishpatim*, judgments. These include all the detailed provisions of civil and criminal law, the rules of reciprocal altruism and distributive justice that make up Judaism's social legislation. Then there are *hukkim*, statutes, such as the laws against eating milk and meat together or wearing clothes of mixed wool and linen. These are sometimes thought of as commands that have no reason. Maimonides rightly dismisses this idea.[19] Essentially, *hukkim* are "laws embedded in nature," and by keeping them we respect the integrity of natural world.[20] So we do not combine animal (wool) and vegetable (linen) textiles, or mix animal life (milk) and animal death (meat). Behind these and other such commands is the idea that God is the creator of biodiversity rather than hybrid uniformity. By observing them we acquire the habits of treating animals with kindness and the environment with care. Judaism's ecological imperative is a delicate balance between "mastering and subduing" nature (Genesis 1) and "serving and protecting" it (Genesis 2). So we have laws against needless waste, the destruction of species, and the despoliation and overexploitation of the environment. The general principle is that we are the guardians of the world for the sake of future generations.

The other great cluster of commands—known as *edot,* or "testimonies"—have to do with our identity as part of a people and its story. So on Passover (*Pesach*) we return to Egypt, eating the bread of affliction and the bitter herbs of slavery; on Pentecost (*Shavuot*) we are at Sinai, hearing the Ten Commandments and sharing in the covenant; and on Tabernacles (*Sukkot*) we reenact the Israelites' journey across the desert with only a hut for a home. The festivals are the supreme transformation of history into memory, from events in the distant past into a personal experience of the present. When I observe the festivals I know, more powerfully than in any other way, that I am not a disconnected atom: I am a letter in the scroll, not yet complete, written by my ancestors, whose past lives on in me.

Beyond these are the three great commands that epitomize Jewish faith. Maimonides famously set out Thirteen Principles of Faith. But, as Rabbi Simeon ben Zemah Duran pointed out in the Middle Ages and Franz Rosenzweig did in modern times, they can be further summarized as three: creation, revelation and redemption.[21] On Shabbat we live creation. Learning Torah we live revelation. Performing acts of *hessed,* covenantal love, we live redemption. We do not philosophize about these things, we enact them. Jewish faith is not primarily about creeds or theologies; it is not faith thought, but faith lived.

No unified field theory will ever finally settle the question of whether or not the universe was created by a personal God. No historical investigation will ever resolve the question of whether, at Sinai, the voice the Israelites heard was real or imagined. No political theory will ever determine whether or not a just and compassionate society is possible. That is not because these things are irrational. It is because they represent truths that can only be made real in life. I can believe that love exists, or I can believe that it is an illusion. Both views are consistent and coherent. I must choose, and that choice will shape my life, leading me to marry or to stay aloof, perhaps having "relationships" but not a total commitment of one life to another. Believing in love, I find it. Disbelieving it, my world is without it. Faith is neither rational nor irrational. It is the courage to make a commitment to an Other, human or divine. It is the determination to turn "ought" into "is." It is the willingness to listen to a voice not my own, and through hearing, find the strength to heal a fractured world. It is truth made real by how I live.

And it works. Throughout the ages, Jews were known for their strong families and communities, their passion for study and the life of the mind, their commitment to helping the poor, the needy and oppressed. Somehow, in oppression they kept their dignity, in persecution their hope. In some of the darkest moments known to man, they stayed human and free. In the Kovno ghetto in the early 1940s, an extraordinary scene took place in the makeshift synagogue. The worshipers already knew the fate in store for them. One morning the leader of prayers stopped in the middle of the service and said, "How can I thank God for my freedom when I am a prisoner facing death? Only a madman could say this prayer now." The rabbi replied softly, "Heaven forbid that we should not say the blessing. Our enemies wish to make us slaves. But though they control our bodies, they do not own our souls. By making this blessing we show that even here we refuse to be defeated. We are free men, temporarily in captivity. That is how we shall live. That, if necessary, is how we shall die."[22]

Judaism led ordinary people to lead extraordinary lives. I profoundly believe that there is nothing special about Jews. The difference, as Menachem Kellner has aptly put it, lies not in the hardware but the software, not in what Jews are but in what they are called on to be.[23] Above all, because they never forgot their ideals, even though they were often powerless to implement them, they were ready for great things when the moment came. Of these, the greatest in modern times was surely the creation of the state of Israel, one of the most unlikely achievements of all time. It could never have happened had we not, for almost two thousand years after the destruction of the second Temple, observed Passover and annually ended the seder by saying, "Next year in Jerusalem." It was this, the world's most ancient unbroken ritual, that moved Moses Hess to write, Theodor Herzl to act, and the great masses of Jews in Eastern Europe to respond to his call. And it is this that constitutes one of the two great challenges of the future.

I noted before that Jews often found it easier to live under the sovereignty of God when their rulers were gentiles than when they were Jews. The other irony is that though

Judaism is an embodied faith—sanctifying the physical and finding God in delight—Jews found it easier to cope with poverty than affluence, with persecution than civil equality and peace. The bad times brought out the best in them, the good times sometimes the worst.

These facts, more than anything else, tell me that far from being over, the Jewish journey has reached its most exciting phase. Today, for the first time in two thousand years, we have a sovereign state in Israel and freedom and equality in the Diaspora. As almost never before we have the chance to succeed where historically Jews failed—in creating a covenantal society in our own land, and a genuine dialogue with humanity elsewhere. I, for one, would not miss it for the world.

Never in history have Jews had so much freedom and affluence, so much diversity and choice, as we do today in the liberal democracies of the West. The average shopper in the average supermarket is confronted with an array of goods that a century ago would have been beyond the dreams of the wealthiest king. Journeys that, a lifetime ago, would have taken months today take hours. We have sent space probes to the most distant planets, photographed the birth of galaxies, fathomed the origins of the universe and decoded the biological structure of life itself. The frontiers of human possibility extend daily. The sheer speed of advance in the twentieth century defies comparison with anything else in the long history of progress. By the beginning of the century there had still been no successful attempt at one of man's oldest dreams: powered flight. Today space shuttles are routine. Ours has been the century of the radio, the television, the laser beam, the computer, the credit card, artificial intelligence, satellite communication, organ transplantation and microsurgery. We have achieved immediate global communication and the instant satisfaction of desires.

But coinciding with these advances, throughout the West, there has been an unprecedented rise in depressive illness, suicide, drug and alcohol abuse, violence and crime. Crime rates have risen 1000 percent in forty years. Since the 1960s, in virtually all the liberal democracies of the West, divorce rates have risen six times, the number of children born outside marriage has risen five times, the number of children living with a single parent has risen three times. These changes have not been without a price. Children are today three to ten times more likely than their parents to need or seek psychiatric help. In the United States, every three hours gun violence takes a child's life; every nine minutes a child is arrested for a drug or alcohol offense; every minute an American teenager has a baby; every twenty-six seconds a child runs away from home.[24]

There is a lovely old Jewish story of a sage who, stroking his beard and looking up from his volume of Talmud, says: "Thank God, things are good." Then he pauses and adds, "But tell me . . . If things are so good, how come they're so bad?" That, surely, is the question of our time. The Jewish answer is that in achieving material abundance we have lost our moral and spiritual bearings. In achieving technical mastery we have lost sight of the question, To what end? Valuing science at the expense of ethics, we have unparalleled knowledge of what is, and unprecedented doubts about what ought to be.

The oldest phenomenon known to history is that civilizations that once seemed invulnerable decline and fall. It has happened to all of them, from Mesopotamia and Egypt to Alexandrian Greece and Imperial Rome, to the Third Reich and the Soviet Union in this century. Why? Few have answered more insightfully than Bertrand Russell, writing of the two ages he most admired:

> What had happened in the great age of Greece happened again in Renaissance Italy. Traditional moral restraints disappeared, because they were seen to be associated with superstition; the liberation from fetters made individuals energetic and creative, producing a rare florescence of genius; but the anarchy and treachery which inevitably resulted from the decay of morals made Italians collectively impotent, and they fell, like the Greeks, under the domination of nations less civilized than themselves but not so destitute of social cohesion.[25]

As societies prosper, so their moral codes become increasingly relaxed. Disciplines that were obviously important at times of adversity come to seem unnecessary in an age of affluence. Prohibitions are abandoned, and the forbidden becomes by turns risqué, avant-garde, and then normal. A sense of common purpose gives way to an ideal of individual self-fulfillment; and at first, nothing happens. Contrary to the dire warnings of the moralists, life continues as normal, because the impact of moral change takes years, sometimes generations, to materialize. Institutions like the family can be abandoned in the short term without apparent loss. By the time social breakdown has become critical, it is already too late to repair. Habits have been lost and self-restraint has been jettisoned. The moral voice itself comes to seem like an unwarranted intrusion into personal freedom. By then a society has reached the stage poignantly described by the Roman writer Livy, at which "we cannot stand either our vices or their cure."[26]

Other civilizations failed because they forgot these difficult truths, so easily lost in affluent times. Jews have never forgotten. They made memory a religious obligation and constantly relived history. They built communities around schools and taught their experience diligently to their children. They never allowed the exhilaration of the present to obscure the lessons of the past or responsibility to the future. That is why Jews were and remain an important voice in the moral conversation of mankind.

We live in an age of anxiety and insecurity. Jews have more than two thousand years of experience in living with insecurity. We live at a time of global communication. The Jewish people are the greatest living example of a global people. We live in a period of moral confusion. So did the prophets, and they left us a moral vision of indelible power. Jews were front-row spectators at the rise and fall of Egypt, Assyria, Babylon, Persia, Greece, Rome. One of the advantages of being a four-thousand-year-old people is that whatever happens, you have been there before. We are called on to be signposts in the wilderness, guides to the perplexed.

Today a view prevails that all ways of life, all lifestyles, are equally valid. Judgment itself is held to be morally wrong because it assaults the principle that each of us should be free to live as we choose. There is a kernel of truth in this—namely that each of us is unique, and there are many different ways of living well. But as for the rest, to use the phrase of the English philosopher Jeremy Bentham, this is "nonsense on stilts." Some ways of life lead on to happiness, others to frustration, loneliness, disappointment and quiet despair. The trouble is that we discover what doesn't work when it is already too late. It is hard in middle age to undo the errors of our youth. Life is an unrepeatable experiment, and if we've taken the wrong turn, it can be hard to go back and begin again. One of the greatest human capacities is rationalization, our almost infinite capacity to justify our errors so that we can be spared the trouble of undoing them.

That is why Jews cared so much about handing on to future generations their own experience and that of their ancestors—experience often bought at great price. A way of life survives not because of power or popularity but because it speaks to something enduring in the human spirit—it calls to the best in us and helps us live it. It creates durable institutions and contains within itself the capacity for growth and renewal. It confers on its members a sense of rightness such that they wish to pass it on to the next generation. There is something about it—a beauty or truth or goodness—that seems to confer majesty on the otherwise tragic human condition. If you find such a tradition, one that has been voluntarily embraced for many centuries, that is a reasonable sign that it contains important truths about what it is to be human. That, for me, is what Judaism is.

Matthew Arnold once said, "As long as the world lasts, all who want to make progress in righteousness will come to Israel for inspiration, as to the people who have had the sense for righteousness most glowing and strongest."[27] Far from having completed its task, it would be fairer to say that a Jewish contribution to civilization has rarely been more urgently needed. For the first time we live in plural societies in which Jews have the opportunity to enter public debate on free and equal terms. And for the first time since the decline and fall of ancient Greece and Rome there is a real battle to be fought between Judaic and neo-pagan ideas of human responsibility, sexuality, the family, the sanctity of human life, the rule of law, the objectivity of moral values, and the ethics of the market and the public square.

We have an ancient story to tell, but one that can never lose its impact so long as human beings still search for meaning and relationship, and graciousness at the heart of collective life, so long as there are still those who see a palace in flames and wish to save it from the fire. This—the long journey of ideas from Abraham to now—has been my answer to the second question: What is it to be a Jew? I now turn to the final question: What went wrong? Why, at the very moment when we are freer than ever before to be Jews, are so many ceasing to be Jews? What is the shadow over Jewish life today?

Part IV

The Future

13

In the Valley of the Shadow

In 1958 A Hassidic rabbi moved to Kew Garden Hills in New York. In those days Kew Garden Hills was not a center of Hassidic life. The appearance of the bearded rabbi in his strange dress—fur hat, dark frock coat—struck an exotic note. The fifties were a time of suburbanization and acculturation. For Jews in particular, America was the New World, an escape from the dark shadows of Europe. The world of Hassidism was foreign to these Americanized Jews, and the rabbi seemed as if he belonged to a different place and time. To their surprise, he had arrived to open a *shteibl*, an old-fashioned synagogue like those in the small townships of Poland and Russia.

A young man in his teens, not very religious, was fascinated by the new arrival. Bored by the services at his local synagogue, he decided to pay the *shteibl* a visit. He found it strange, a little outlandish, but intriguing. After the service ended, the rabbi came over to him. He told him that Pesach was coming soon. And on Pesach you need a child to ask the four questions that begin the seder service. He, the rabbi, did not have a child who could ask. All he had was a baby daughter a few months old. Would the young man be kind enough to join the rabbi and his wife for the seder and ask the questions?

He went. He was surprised to see, between the rabbi and his wife, a large baby carriage. They had brought their daughter, now sleeping, to the table to be present at the recitation of the Haggadah. The seder began, and the young man asked the questions. The rabbi began reading the familiar Hebrew words of reply. Half an hour into the seder, the baby woke and started to cry. The rabbi asked permission of his wife and guest to leave the table for a while. He took the baby in his arms and went into the bedroom. The young man could hear the rabbi soothing her, dancing gently around the room, and singing a song over and over again. The song was in Yiddish and the young man did not understand its words. But soon the baby stopped crying and went to sleep. The rabbi returned and the seder continued. There the story might have ended, but it didn't.

Intrigued by the rabbi and his tenderness for the baby, the young man began to find out where he came from, what his story was. The rabbi, it transpired, came from Warsaw. He had been studying there when the Second World War broke out and had just married. Like all the other Jews, he and his wife found themselves prisoners in the ghetto. Conditions were terrible and worsened week by week. There was starvation, disease; people lay dead and unburied in the streets.

The rabbi was soon transported to Treblinka, and from there he was taken to other concentration camps. He still had his number tattooed on his arm. His wife, too, was taken to a concentration camp, where Nazi doctors used her for their medical experiments. Somehow they both survived. After the war, emaciated, half alive, they were taken to DP camps, where they stayed until they were able to come to America.

Because of what had been done to her, his wife was told by American doctors that she had been made infertile. The couple would not be able to have a child. But they refused to give up hope. They visited specialists, went through years of exploring all medical avenues. More than ten years later, at last it happened. By a miracle—so it seemed to them—she conceived. They had a child. This was the child the rabbi had taken in his arms.

But it wasn't this that changed the young man's life. What did change it, leading the young man to become religious—and eventually a rabbi, which he is today—was the slow, dawning understanding of the words the rabbi had sung to the baby as he danced with her in his arms, what they meant and what they signified. What were they, the words sung over and over again to a baby by a rabbi who had lived through the Warsaw ghetto and Treblinka and passed through the gates of hell? *Zis gut zu zein a Yid, Zis gut zu zein a Yid.* "It's good to be a Jew. It's good to be a Jew."[1]

I have stood at Auschwitz and felt my blood turn to ice. I have passed through the gates of Stammlager Auschwitz with their inscription that mocks all meaning, *Arbeit macht frei* ("Work makes you free"). I have walked through the killing fields of Auschwitz-Birkenau, where whole Jewish communities from Sweden to Greece to Hungary were gassed and burned and turned to ash. I stood in the halls that still hold the last possessions of the victims—mountains of suitcases, piles of toothbrushes, and hundreds of thousands of shoes, worn, battered but still collected and kept—and realized that for the Nazis nothing was so valueless as to be thrown away, except Jewish life. A million shoes saved. A million lives destroyed. Then I felt the silence that swallows words and robs them of their meaning.

Judaism has its silences, Elie Wiesel once said, but we do not speak about them.[2] After the Holocaust there was one of the great silences of Jewish history. A third of world Jewry had gone up in flames. Entire universes—the bustling Jewish townships of Eastern Europe, the talmudic academies, the courts of the Jewish mystics, the Yiddish-speaking masses, the urbane Jews of Germany, the Jews of Poland who had lived among their gentile neighbors for eight hundred years, the legendary synagogues and houses of study— all were erased. A guard at Auschwitz, testifying at the Nuremberg trials, explained that at the height of the genocide, when the camp was turning ten thousand Jews into smoke, children were thrown into the furnaces alive. When the destruction was over, a pillar of cloud marked the place where Europe's Jews had once been. Today, I cannot walk through the streets of Germany and Austria and Poland without feeling that I am in the midst of ghosts.

In the Warsaw ghetto there lived and died a great and saintly rabbi, a Hassidic Rebbe, Rabbi Kalonymous Shapiro. Throughout the years 1941–1943 he taught his disciples, and wrote down the addresses he delivered in a book. Knowing he would not survive, he buried the book under the ground. It was discovered after the war. As the weeks went by, Rabbi Shapiro saw his community, his friends, his family, his children, one by one, taken to the extermination camps. And still he taught, though with greater and greater pain, until one day he told his disciples that God Himself was weeping, and if a single tear were to escape from heaven to earth, it would destroy the world.[3]

As long as there is a Jewish people, we will remember. We will weep, and there will be no comfort. Where was God at Auschwitz? Sooner or later this was the question I had to ask, because the Holocaust still casts its shadow over Jewish life. The Jewish journey from then to now, from Abraham and Sarah to our time, passes not once but many times through the valley of the shadow of death. Where, when His people were dying, was God? Why, when His people were calling to Him, was He silent?

In the book that bears his name, Job asks questions of heaven, among the most searing ever written. Why are the righteous afflicted? Why do the innocent suffer? God answers only by way of other questions. "Where were you when I laid the foundations of the universe?"[4] It took courage to ask Job's questions, greater courage to include this deeply troubling book in the Hebrew Bible, and greater courage still to refuse all easy answers. But the question was born long before Job. In the beginning there were Cain and Abel, the first two human children:

Now Abel kept flocks, and Cain worked the soil.
In the course of time Cain brought some of the fruits of the soil
as an offering to the Lord.
But Abel brought fat portions from some of the firstborn of his
flock.
The Lord looked with favor on Abel and his offering, but on
Cain and his offering He did not look with favor.
So Cain was very angry, and his face was downcast.
Then the Lord said to Cain, "Why are you angry?
Why is your face downcast?
If you do what is right, will you not be accepted?
But if you do not do what is right, sin is crouching
at your door.
It desires to have you,
But you must master it."

Now Cain said to his brother Abel, "Let's go out to the
field . . ."
And while they were in the field, Cain attacked his brother
Abel and killed him.
Then the Lord said to Cain, "Where is your brother Abel?"
"I don't know," he answered. "Am I my brother's keeper?"
The Lord said, "What have you done? Listen! Your brother's
blood cries out to Me from the ground."[5]

Where was God when Cain killed Abel? Given the biblical text and its assumptions, it is a question we cannot avoid. God knew of Cain's murderous intentions in advance and warned him of them. Moreover, Abel and Cain were engaged in an act of religious worship, the first recorded offering to God. God might even be said to be the instigator of the conflict, by not favoring Cain's offering. Where was God, when He might have intervened?

To this there is one answer. We have been traveling with it since we first met Abraham and his cry at the injustice of the world. Abraham, says the *midrash,* saw a palace in flames, God's order threatened by the chaos of mankind. To the question, "Where is God?" God replies with a question of his own, "Where are you?"—his first words to Adam and Eve, and to Job. Jewish faith did not die in this question; it was born in it.

Only now, perhaps, can we appreciate the depth and pathos of Jewish faith. For what are the alternatives? We can deny the reality of either God or evil. Then the dissonance would disappear, and we could live at peace with the world. But if God exists and evil is an illusion, then Auschwitz is justified. We may not know why, but this we know, that from the vantage point of heaven there was a reason for it and we must accept it as God's unfathomable will. The alternative is that God does not exist, and thus the universe is blind to our hopes, deaf to our cries, indifferent to our existence. In such a world there is no reason not to expect an Auschwitz. Jewish faith is the principled refusal to accept either answer, because each would allow us to live at peace with the world, and it is morally impossible to live at peace with a world that contains an Auschwitz.

It took faith to create mankind.[6] The moral bond—the covenant—is a relationship between free agents, each respecting the integrity of the other. In seeing the moral bond as the personal reality of the universe, Jews could not but believe in a free God who creates free human beings. Free human beings are the only creations capable of committing evil. And since they are free, God does not prevent them from committing evil. God, who seeks only justice and righteousness and peace in the world, must therefore create the possibility of violence and torture and bloodshed in the world.

There is no escaping this dilemma, even in Heaven itself. There is no weighing in the balance of good against evil, evil against good, to decide whether in the long run the universe is better with or without man. For no good deed cancels out the taking of a single innocent life. Good inspires, it consoles, but it does not compensate. There are only two choices: not to create man and thus leave God alone in eternity with no other being capable of recognizing Him in freedom; or to have faith and create man. God had faith, and made man. This simple truth, reverberating through time with its consequences, seems to me more profound than all theodicies, all attempts to explain. This is not the best of possible worlds, or the worst of possible worlds. It is the only possible world in which the I of God meets the Thou of man.

The most profound of all modern thinkers was the German philosopher Friedrich Nietzsche, who wrote in the second half of the nineteenth century. From time to time he expressed admiration for Jews—he once called them "the most remarkable nation of world history."[7] But he consistently opposed Judaism for a most unusual reason: not because Jews rejected Christianity, but because Jews had given birth to Christianity. Judaism was wrong, he said, because it was the inversion of all natural instincts. It found God in right, not might; in compassion, not ruthlessness; in humility, not aristocratic disdain. It represented all the things he despised: "pity, the kind and helping hand, the warm heart, patience, industriousness, humility, friendliness."[8] He termed these the "slave virtues" and thought that those who embraced them were weak and envious. The true ethic was the precise opposite, the "will to power."

Nietzsche was the first writer to speak about "the death of God," meaning the end of that view of the world that we call the Judaic, or Judeo-Christian, ethic. It is no accident that, seventy years after he wrote about the death of God, his nation was setting in motion its plan for the death of the people of God.[9] Nietzsche was right: Judaism is the negation of the will to power. If God exists, then the moral law exists. If the moral law exists, then conscience exists; and if conscience exists, there are limits to power. Not for nothing was the covenant with mankind made in the words: "Whoever sheds the blood of man, by man shall his blood be shed, for in the image of God has God made man."[10] The abolition of God leads inexorably to the abolition of man. For only as the image of God is human life not part of nature, but sacred. Hitler was not wrong when he called conscience a Jewish invention. That is one reason why I am a Jew. A world, a nation, a religion that does not have room for Judaism or Jews is a world, a nation, a religion that does not have room for humanity.

Jewish faith is not about believing the world to be other than it is. It is not about ignoring the evil, the darkness and the pain. It is about courage, endurance and the capacity to hold fast to ideals even when they are ignored by others. It is the ability to see the world for what it is and yet still believe that it could be different. It is about not giving up, not letting go. Faith is what the Song of Songs calls "the love which is stronger than death."[11] That faith is expressed whenever we have the courage to live as Jews and bring new Jewish life into the world.

Abraham, Moses and the prophets taught not a Jewish truth but a human truth. God has chosen only one dwelling place in this universe and that is the human heart. Whenever we banish God from the heart, tragic things happen. When rulers set themselves in place of God, they begin by taking other people's liberty and end by taking other people's lives. There is a direct line from tyranny to idolatry to bloodshed. Our greatest, our only, defense is the knowledge that above all earthly powers is the supreme king of kings, God, who has endowed all human beings with His image. No absolute ruler has ever succeeded in extinguishing that spark from the souls of a people. That is why all tyrannies have failed and will always fail. That is why this small people who predicated their existence on the most fragile of things—a vision, a book, a faith—still live, while every great power that sought their destruction, from Egypt to Persia to the Third Reich and the Soviet Union, are no more.

In our century, after the Holocaust, a ravaged, devastated people came back to the land of Israel and there built one of the great states of the modern world. Out of the wilderness they built farms and forests. In place of the totalitarian states from which many of them came, they framed a democracy. From a small population, they created an army of invincible courage. In place of Jerusalem "in mourning and in ruins"[12] they created a Jerusalem built "as a city that is closely joined together."[13] They made the Hebrew language, the language of the Bible, live again. They built *yeshivot*, citadels of Jewish learning, so that the streets of Jerusalem would once again echo with the sound of ancient learning. They brought Jewish communities, threatened by persecution, to safety. Together they brought about the collective resurrection of the Jewish people from the shadow of death to the land of life. Today when Jews sing of Israel, they say *od lo avdah tikvatenu*, "Our hope is not destroyed."

If you were to ask what our response to the Holocaust should be, I would say this: Marry and have children, bring new Jewish life into the world, build schools, make communities, have faith in God who had faith in man and make sure that His voice is heard wherever evil threatens. Pursue justice, defend the defenseless, have the courage to be different and fight for the dignity of difference. Recognize the image of God in others, and defeat hate with love. Twice a year, on *Yom ha-Shoah* and the Ninth of Av, sit and mourn for those who died and remember them in your prayers. But most of all, continue to live as Jews.

When I stand today in Jerusalem, or in a Jewish school, or see a Jewish couple under the wedding canopy, or see parents at the Shabbat table blessing their children, there are times when I am overcome with tears, not in sadness nor in joy, but in awe at this people who came face to face with the angel of death and refused to give it a final victory. The Jewish people live, and still bear witness to the living God.

14

Ambivalence and Assimilation

ONE OF THE MOST TELLING REMARKS ever made about modern Jewish identity was delivered by Groucho Marx. "I wouldn't belong," he once said, "to a club that would have me as a member." In that one sentence are all the aspirations and fears, the longing for acceptance and the expectation of rejection—all the ambivalence of the twentieth century Jew. The late Shlomo Carlebach, rabbi and folksinger who spent a lifetime talking to students on campus, once said: "We get to talking about religion and I ask people what they are. If someone says, 'I'm a Catholic,' I know he's a Catholic. If someone says, 'I'm a Protestant,' I know she's a Protestant. If someone says, 'I'm just a human being,' I know that's a Jew." The comedian Jackie Mason says, "Jews come to my shows. They laugh at my jokes. Then they shake their heads and say, '*Too Jewish.*'" These are injured voices, coming from a world of conflicted identity. We laugh because otherwise we would cry.

For the past century, perhaps for much longer, a deep ambivalence has cast its shadow over Jewish life. Since the First Crusade, in 1096, Jews had periodically been attacked and murdered for being Jews. In the Middle Ages, Spain alone seemed to offer a refuge. Then it too turned against the Jews. In the late eighteenth century, a new era began with an unprecedented promise. In 1789 the French Revolution heralded the secular state, with its Declaration of the Rights of Man and of the Citizen. It began with these words: "All men are born, and remain, free and equal in rights." Never had hope burned more brightly. Enlightenment would end religious prejudice. Emancipation would give equality to Jews. The disillusionment, when it came, was bitter.

Far from disappearing, anti-Jewish sentiment mutated into a new and terrible form. In 1879 it was given a name: anti-Semitism. What was it, and in what sense was it new? Hatred and persecution of Jews goes back to biblical times. It was continued by the Greeks and Romans. It found a special place in Christian theology. There were, however, two things distinctive about modern anti-Semitism.

The first is that it took place in a secular culture. Jews in the past were disliked for what they believed and what they did. In Christian and Islamic societies they stood apart from the dominant faith. Strictly speaking, this was not anti-Semitism but anti-Judaism. It was only when politics were secularized and prejudice could no longer be given a religious justification, that hatred became racial. Jews were disliked not for what they believed but for what they were; not for their faith but for the mere fact of their birth. Far from curing prejudice, secularization gave it a new and absolute character.

The second was that it placed Jews in a double bind. In the past Jews faced a clear and simple choice. Even in the dark days of the Spanish expulsion, Jews were given an alternative: convert and stay, or remain Jewish and leave. Emancipation seemed to offer a secular equivalent of the same choice. "Become like us," went the liberal argument, "and we will treat you like us." But the invitation was fate-fully deceptive, and the more Jews tried to be like everyone else, they more they were reminded that they were different. What others simply were, Jews labored to become, and the harder they tried, the more conspicuously they failed.

Anti-Semitism was irrational and inescapable. Jews were derided as communists and capitalists. They were criticized for remaining aloof and for being overeager to join. They were seen as poor and powerless, and as rich and powerful. Some, like Voltaire, complained that they clung to an ancient and superstitious faith;[1] others, like T. S. Eliot, that they were freethinkers who had no faith.[2] Anti-Semitism was protean, constantly mutating into new forms and providing an object for new fears. It could not be defeated by rational argument because it had no rational basis. But it was murderous in its intent and its effect, and we still bear its scars.

However, there is a secondary effect of hatred: It can sometimes enter the minds of those who are hated.[3] Jews not only began to behave in a new way, they began to see themselves in a new way. In the past they had been different and were proud to be different. Now they were embarrassed to be different and went to great lengths to minimize the fact. They began to see themselves as others saw them. Eventually they discovered that this was sometimes very negative indeed. Fatefully, Jews became ambivalent about themselves. Thus the conflicted modern Jewish identity was born.

There have been two tragedies in modern Jewish life. The first was external and physical: the rise of racial anti-Semitism, from the Kishinev pogroms in Russia to the Dreyfus Affair in France to the Final Solution and the death camps in Nazi Germany. The second was internal and spiritual. Anti-

Semitism did more than threaten, and eventually take, the lives of Jews. It left a trace in the Jewish soul. Jews began to see themselves not as the people loved by God but rather as the people hated by gentiles. That turned Jewishness back from a faith to a fate, from a positive destiny to a tragic misfortune. Mordecai Kaplan once wrote: "Before the beginning of the nineteenth century all Jews regarded Judaism as a privilege; since then most Jews have come to regard it as a burden."[4] Those words were written in 1934, before the Holocaust. Since then they have not ceased to be true.

From earliest times Jewish history was often fraught with tears. Pharaoh, Amalek, Haman and Nebuchadnezzar form part of a long litany of persecution, summarized in a famous passage in the Passover Haggadah: "It was not one man alone who rose against us to destroy us. In every generation there are those who rise against us to destroy us." Yet there is a crucial difference between the ancient and modern experience and its impact on Jewish identity. In the past, suffering was interpreted in a theological framework. It belonged to the terms of the covenant. A prophet such as Amos could say in the name of God, "You alone have I singled out of all the families of the earth—that is why I will call you to account for all your iniquities."[5] The very fact of national distress was accompanied by a promise and a hope: if Jews returned to God, God would return to them. It could even serve as the basis of a strange form of pride. Writing in the eleventh century, Judah Halevi could argue that Jews among the nations were like the heart among the limbs of a body, more susceptible to illness because more sensitive than any other organ.[6] At the very least, Jewish suffering had a coherent inner logic. It confirmed the destiny of this singular people, unlike others, outside the norms of history, often wayward and severely punished for its backslidings, yet part of a drama whose final act is homecoming. Judaism is the systematic rejection of tragedy in the name of hope.

What made modern anti-Semitism different from its precursors was not only that it was secularized; so too were its victims. It occurred precisely at that point in history where Jews had placed their faith, not in (religious) redemption but in (secular) emancipation. This may have been inevitable. At last politics was promising to deliver what centuries of prayer had not: civil rights, social equality, a place in the mainstream of European culture. But the result was to leave large swathes of Jewry bereft of an interpretive scheme within which to understand what was happening to them and to integrate it within their self-image. Part of the tacit bargain of secular politics was that Jews would begin to see themselves as others saw them. But this image, it turned out, was shatteringly negative. Already by 1882, the Russian-Jewish writer Judah Leib Pinsker could speak of the Jew as a ghost among the living.[7] Sixty years later, metaphor was beginning to become fact.

We have moved well beyond the Holocaust. But when a collective crisis of this magnitude affects almost an entire people—especially when the reality turned out to be worse than their worst nightmare—the aftermath lingers on. We are still, today, uneasier about who we are than any other group in the Western world. There is nothing natural about the rates of outmarriage in the Diaspora, or the extent of secularization in Israel. They are the residual traces of a profound disturbance, as yet unexorcised, within the Jewish soul.

In many cases our parents and grandparents were not absolutely sure that they wanted their children to be Jews. They didn't want them to marry out, but they also didn't want them to stand out, to be conspicuous. They wanted them to be secular *marranos,* outwardly like everyone else, inwardly and privately Jews. They wanted them to be visible as human beings but invisible as Jews. They were haunted by the specter of anti-Semitism, and they were not wrong to be. But it left them deeply conflicted. They were Jews, but they were dedicated to proving that Jews are no different from anyone else. And we, whether we know it or not, have inherited that deeply conflicted world.

This, I believe, is what lies behind the three voices with which I began this book—the three distinguished Jews who wrote to the students and were unable to say anything positive about what being Jewish meant to them. The dissonance between their views and those of the non-Jews I quoted is not accidental. Behind it lies a long and painful history of more than a century of anti-Semitism that has left its mark on the Jewish soul. That history stands like a barrier between us and our past, preventing us from understanding who we are.

It cannot continue. Ambivalence cannot sustain an identity. It creates a tension that is ultimately resolved—perhaps generations later—by children walking away and ceasing to be Jews, and that is what is happening now. This is a tragedy for many reasons, most of all because it makes no sense in terms of where we are and who we are. In Israel we have a home. In the Diaspora we have freedom and equality. Attitudes that were understandable two generations ago are, by now, profoundly dysfunctional and utterly unrelated to the world in which we live. We have to face and resolve this crisis of ambivalence. A half-century after the Holocaust and the birth of Israel, we are perhaps the first generation that can.

. . .

And yet something remains terribly wrong in Jewish life to-day. In 1991 a survey was published in the United States showing that among young Jews, 57 percent had married non-Jews.[8] This figure sent shock waves throughout the Jewish world, giving rise to books with such alarmist titles as *Vanishing Diaspora* and *The Vanishing American Jew.*[9]

Outmarriage has been a problem of Jewish life since the very beginning of our history. Abraham was concerned that Isaac should not marry into the local Canaanite population.[10] Isaac and Rebecca were distressed when Esau married two Hittite women.[11] Moses delivered warnings against intermar-riage.[12] Ezra and Nehemiah, returning to Israel after the Babylonian exile, instituted drastic measures against those who had been "unfaithful to our God by marrying foreign women from the peoples around us."[13] The rabbis of Mish-naic times enacted decrees against behavior that might lead to intermarriage.[14] So the problem is not new. It is perhaps the oldest we have faced. But never so suddenly and on this scale.

In the United States itself, intermarriage in the 1920s af-fected no more than one percent of the Jewish population. A study in 1944 yielded a figure of 2.6 per cent. Until the 1960s it remained at or below 6 percent. But in the first half of that decade the rate jumped to 17.4 percent and by 1971 it had risen to 31.7 percent.[15] The figure of 57 percent in 1991 meant that the rate had risen almost ten times in less than thirty years. The Jewish community in the United States, the largest in the world, is disappearing faster than any other since the Lost Ten Tribes vanished from the pages of history more than two and a half thousand years ago. The same is happening, slightly less dramatically, in Britain. The British Jewish community, estimated in the 1950s to number some 450,000 individuals, had declined by the late 1990s to 280,000. This means that the Jewish community has lost ten Jews a day, every day, for more than forty years.[16]

What was remarkable, even unique about Jews in the past was that they did not assimilate. They preserved their traditions and customs and way of life. Jews were different and stayed different. They kept their identity, and so their communities did not disappear. Perhaps what is happening now has happened before. In fifteenth-century Spain many Jews converted to Christianity. They did so in Germany at the end of the eighteenth century, and in Russia in the nineteenth. In prewar Vienna, thousands of Jews every year declared themselves *konfessionsloss*, "of no religion." Already in 1927 in France, Edmond Fleg had written his response to assimilation, *Why I am a Jew*, in which he asked of the next generation, "Will there still be Jews?"[17] So the problem is not new. But in Fleg's day Jews were leaving Judaism because of anti-Semitism—quite simply, it was unsafe to remain a Jew. His whole book is haunted by the ghost of the Dreyfus Affair more than thirty years earlier, and the specter it exposed of anti-Jewish feeling at all levels of French society. Fleg himself had drifted far from Judaism, had toyed with conversion to Christianity, until he realized that this too would not solve the problem. A Jew, even one who had left his faith, would never be accepted as a Frenchman, so let him remain a Jew. Looking back at his work, it is impossible not to be moved by its sincerity and its tragedy. Fleg never had Jewish grandchildren: his children were killed in the early days of the Second World War. By the time his book was published in English, in 1943, the Final Solution was gathering pace and Jewish life in Europe was coming close to extinction.

In the past, Jews left Judaism to avoid prejudice and discrimination. Today, in countries where intermarriage rates are highest, there is no terror and no threat—Jews have freedom and equality and they are among the most highly educated and upwardly mobile of any ethnic or religious group. A century and a half ago Heinrich Heine, the Jewish poet, called baptism his "entry ticket to European culture." Today no culture needs an entry ticket, least of all one that is bought at the price of ceasing to be a Jew.

•   Perhaps the explanation is simpler. Perhaps Jews wanted to leave all along, but simply did not have the chance. Could it be that today's high rates of outmarriage represent not the failure of anything, but the success of a truly tolerant society? At last Jews are not locked—by prejudice or hostility—into the room marked Judaism, and they can enter the broad spaces of anonymity. But for millennia, longer than any other minority people, Jews stayed true to their identity. They resisted the blandishments of Christianity and Islam. They preferred poverty and persecution to acceptance bought at the price of denying who they were. Time and again—in twelfth-century Islam, fifteenth-century Spain, in the days of Martin Luther—Jews held firm to their faith despite every inducement to do otherwise.

Could it be that today's society has made Jewish identity superfluous? For two thousand years, Jews represented difference. As the prophet Balaam said, they were "a people that dwells alone, not reckoned among the nations."[18] Perhaps today the very concept of difference has ceased to have a role in the diverse, pluralist, multicultural societies of the West, where everyone is different, everyone a minority. Might it be, not that Jews are ceasing to be Jews, but that everyone else is becoming Jewish? No: if anything, the liberal democracies of the West are abandoning the very values that were once known as the Judeo-Christian tradition. The family, the community, the sanctity of human life, the concept of an objective set of moral values, the idea of a covenant linking the present to the past—these are ideals in danger, not reigning orthodoxies. Society is not becoming more Jewish but manifestly and rapidly less so. Nor is the Jewish flight from Judaism a mere reflection of what is happening in other faiths. For at least half a century, American Jews have scored measurably lower on indices of religious belief and conduct than their non-Jewish neighbors. A Gallup poll in December 1991 asked New Yorkers, "How important is religion in your life?" Seventy-four percent of blacks, 57 percent of white Catholics, and 47 percent of white Protestants answered, "Very important," as against 34 percent of Jews.[19] Four out of ten Americans claim to attend religious services weekly, but only one in ten of America's Jews.[20]

That is the tragedy. Jews, once the most loyal of all nations, have become the most casually indifferent to our past. Once the most God-intoxicated of all peoples, we have become the most secular. Jews who once found peace in the candles of a Shabbat table and the Divine presence in simple deeds and ordinary lives, have become the restless seekers of salvation in every faith except our own—from sects to sex, from Scientology to psychotherapy, from Buddhism to New Age mysticism. Homeless in the world, our ancestors were at home in their faith. Today, at home everywhere, we have become paradigms of the homeless mind.

Might it be, most seriously, that the Jewish people are in revolt against the very terms of their destiny? We were—we defined ourselves as—the nation of the covenant, a chosen people, a people loved by God. Is it possible that after more than a century of anti-Semitism, culminating in the Holocaust, Jews are no longer ready to place their trust in God? At the most agonizing moment of our history, we cried and there was no answer. We prayed and there was no reply.

I do not share this reaction, but I understand it. Yet this too cannot be the explanation. The explosion of intermarriage did not take place after the Holocaust. It is happening now, more than fifty years later. Those years have made a crucial difference; in them the State of Israel came into being. After a lapse of almost two thousand years Jews have at last recovered their national sovereignty. Rescued from every place where they faced persecution—Iran, Iraq, Yemen, Romania, Russia, Ethiopia, Syria—Jews find themselves once again in the Holy Land. For the first time since the destruction of the second Temple, every Jew has a home in the sense defined by the poet Robert Frost, who said that home is where "when you have to go there, they have to let you in."

For generations our ancestors prayed, more in hope than expectation, "Sound the great shofar for our freedom, raise the signal to gather our exiles, and gather us together from the four corners of the earth." We have lived to witness the answer to that prayer. In my lifetime I have seen events of which the great prophets of return—Isaiah, Jeremiah, Ezekiel—could only dream. None of this negates the Holocaust. But it allows us to move beyond it. The Jewish people no longer live in the valley of the shadow of death. Overwhelmingly today Jews live in Israel and the United States, countries free of the legacy of that dark past. Even in Germany and the former Soviet Union, the two countries that did most to seek the extinction of Jews and Judaism, there is a freedom to practice our faith that we did not know before.

What is wrong in Jewish life today is that we have forgotten *Zis gut zu zein a Yid,* "It's good to be a Jew."

15

This Is Ours

THE EPISODE IN WHICH the Jewish people got its name—Israel—is among the most enigmatic in the Bible. Jacob is returning home after an absence of many years. He had left because his brother Esau was threatening to kill him. Esau was aggrieved—Jacob had taken his birthright and, in disguise, stolen his blessing. Now they are about to meet again, and Jacob is overcome by fear. He divides his family into two, so that if there is a battle, at least some will survive. He prays to God. He sends Esau gifts in the hope that they may placate him. He avails himself of all the options. If the gifts fail, prayer will help. If prayer fails, he is prepared for war. But some uneasiness still haunts him. He moves his family across the river. As he is coming back he meets a stranger:

> Jacob was left alone, and a man wrestled with him till daybreak. When the man saw that he could not overcome him, he touched the socket of Jacob's hip so that his hip was wrenched as he wrestled with the man. Then the man said, "Let me go, for it is daybreak." But Jacob replied, "I will not let you go unless you bless me." The man asked him, "What is your

name?" "Jacob," he answered. Then the man said, "Your name will no longer be Jacob, but Israel, because you have struggled with God and with men and have overcome."[1]

With whom was Jacob struggling? With a man? An angel? With God? What does the encounter signify? Why was it *this* moment that gave its name not only to Jacob but to the Jewish people? The Bible clearly wishes us to understand that the encounter is in some way emblematic of the entire Jewish people. The source of our name, it symbolizes our collective identity. So the wrestling match between Jacob and his mysterious adversary is not just something that happened once long ago. We are to understand that it will recur at critical moments throughout Jewish history as an intimation of who we are.

There are many commentaries on and interpretations of this passage. What clues, though, does the Bible itself offer that might help us decipher the mystery? What else does it tell us about Jacob? It describes a series of events, all of which cast light on how Jacob saw himself. We know that when he was younger, he bought Esau's birthright. Later he dressed in Esau's clothes, told his blind father that he was Esau, and under that pretense took Esau's blessing. His very name, Jacob, was given to him because, when he was born, he was holding on to Esau's heel. Together these amount to a psychologically striking proposition. Jacob was the child who wanted to be his brother. Esau was the first-born; he was strong and a hunter, the child whom his father loved. Jacob, who was none of these things, wanted to be Esau, not Jacob the younger, the weaker and the apparently unloved.

If only he had known the full story, what grief might he have spared his brother and himself! Reading the biblical text carefully we make a remarkable discovery. The real blessing intended for him was not the one he took while pretending to be Esau: "May God give you from the dew of the heavens and the fat of the earth."[2] That was a blessing of physical prosperity. The blessing meant for Jacob was the one given to him later as Jacob, when Isaac was distressed that Esau had married into the local Hittite tribes. It was then that Isaac blessed him with these words: "May God Almighty bless you and make you fruitful and increase your numbers until you become a community of peoples. May He give you and your descendants the blessing of Abraham, so that you may take possession of the land where you now live as a stranger, the land God gave to Abraham."[3] Children and a land: these throughout Genesis and Jewish history have been the covenantal promise. This blessing had all along been destined for Jacob. The irony is overwhelming. Jacob's striving to be Esau was unnecessary. To acquire the blessing, he needed to be not Esau, but himself.

Alone at night many years later, about to meet Esau again after long estrangement, Jacob faces the defining crisis of his life. Who is he? Is he still the man who wants to be Esau? Or is he capable of becoming himself? On this psychological drama the entire course of Jewish history will turn. Jacob cannot escape. Tomorrow he will stand face to face with his brother. Now or never he must decide who he is.

There are many opinions as to the identity of Jacob's mysterious adversary. The simplest and deepest is that it was Jacob himself, and that his greatest struggle was internal. Would he spend his life wishing he were someone else,

or would he at last be content to be who he was? His struggle ended when he was able to let go of all the things he had
clung to in the past. According to this reading, Jacob became Israel when he learned to be proud to be Jacob. No
longer holding on to Esau's heel, his blessing, his identity,
his name, Jacob finally conquered his sense of inadequacy
and learned to be himself. For the first time he could meet
his brother without envy, deception or fear. The next morning, the brothers meet and the conflict between them
seems to have disappeared. They kiss, speak in friendship,
and each goes his way in peace. If Jacob has the courage to
be Jacob, then he has conquered his fear of Esau.

This scene has often replayed itself at critical junctures
in Jewish history. Time and again Jews confronted nations
larger than themselves, more powerful, more secure, more
at home in the world—ancient Egypt and Persia, Greece
and Rome, Europe of the Enlightenment—and each time
there were Jews who were not sure they wanted to be Jews.
They assimilated or Hellenized or secularized. Each of
these encounters was a collective crisis of Jewish identity, a
paralyzing self-doubt. Jews did not want to belong to the
club that would have them as a member. They were Jacobs
who did not want to be Jacob.

The result was tragic. Living by someone else's identity
creates confusion, anxiety and insecurity. The more assimilated a Jewish community is, the more haunted it is by anti-
Semitism. It is one thing to fear objective danger. It is
another to have the anxiety that comes from not knowing
who you are. As long as Jacob saw himself as Esau, he
threatened Esau and felt threatened by him. Only when he
became Israel could the two brothers, each secure in his
own identity, meet as equals and part as friends.

At such critical points in our history, the Jewish people has had to make a conscious effort to reaffirm its identity. On each occasion it has had to undergo its own equivalent of the wrestling match which gave Israel its name. Jacob became Israel when he learned to be proud to be Jacob. We must learn to be proud to be his children.

In his insightful and engaging book *The Ordeal of Civility*, John Murray Cuddihy describes what he calls "the primal scene" in the life of Sigmund Freud. This is how Freud himself describes it:

> At that point I was brought up against the event in my youth whose power was still being shown in all these emotions and dreams. I may have been ten or twelve years old, when my father began to take me with him on his walks and to reveal to me in his talk his views upon things in the world we live in. Thus it was, on one such occasion that he told me a story to show me how much better things were now than they had been in his days. "When I was a young man," he said, "I went for a walk one Saturday in the streets of your birthplace [Freiberg, in Moravia]; I was well dressed, and had a new cap on my head. A Christian came up to me and with a single blow knocked off my cap into the mud and shouted: 'Jew! Get off the pavement!'" "And what did you do?" I asked. "I went into the roadway and picked up my cap," was his quiet reply. This struck me as unheroic conduct on the part of the big strong man who was holding the little boy by the hand.[4]

Freud goes on to describe his disappointment and shame at his father's weak response. Cuddihy relates this moment to much of Freud's work—his ambivalent relationship with Jews and non-Jews, his theory of the Oedipus complex, and his strange assertion in *Moses and Monotheism* that Moses was not a Jew but an Egyptian. Is this reading too much into too little? Or is it actually the case that the course of our lives is often tilted this way or that by such moments, which lend a particular color—proud or shameful, confident or embarrassed—to our image of ourselves?

I recall three such primal scenes that made a difference to my own life. The first was almost the mirror image of Freud's. Once, when I was a child, my family was on holiday in a little coastal town in the south of England. It was Shabbat and we had just left the synagogue and were walking back for lunch. Behind us, another member of the congregation came rushing up and pointed to the *yarmulka* I was wearing. He said to my father, "Your son has forgotten to take his *yarmulka* off." This was in the days when it was not done to wear overt signs of your Jewishness in public. The old dictum "Be a Jew at home and a man in the street" was still in force. By walking down the road with my head-covering I was committing a solecism, and our friend from the synagogue assumed, not unnaturally, that I was unaware of it. He meant it kindly. He was simply trying to save me from embarrassment, much as if my shirttail had been hanging out. For once my father got angry and replied, "No child of mine will ever be ashamed to be Jewish in public." And we continued on our way. It was not a very tactful response, but it taught me—as perhaps no more formal lesson could—never to be ashamed of who I was.

• The second event took place several years later. I was a student on my own personal journey, searching for an understanding of Judaism. My travels took me to New York, where for the first time I met one of the world's great Jewish leaders, the Lubavitcher Rebbe, Rabbi Menachem Mendel Schneersohn. We met and talked, and I was deeply impressed. For the next few days I was in a state of turmoil. I now felt the pull of Jewish spirituality as never before. But could I really embrace this life, which seemed so narrow after the broad expanses of Western culture? Where in this world was there a place for Mozart and Milton, Beethoven and Shakespeare? Where in this focused existence was there room for the glittering achievements of the European mind? I wrote a note to the Rebbe and told him of my conflict. I wanted to live more fully as a Jew, but at the same time I was reluctant to give up my love of art and literature, music and poetry, most of which had been created by non-Jews and had nothing to do with Judaism.

The Rebbe wrote me back an answer in the form of a parable. Imagine, he said, two people, both of whom have spent their lives carrying stones. One carries rocks, the other diamonds. Now imagine that they are both asked to carry a consignment of emeralds. To the man who has spent his life transporting rocks, emeralds too are rocks—a burden, a weight. After a lifetime, that is how he sees what he is asked to carry. But to the man who has spent his life carrying diamonds, emeralds too are precious stones—different, to be sure, but still things of value and beauty. So it is, he said, with different civilizations and faiths. To the person for whom faith is just a burden, so too are other faiths. He does not value his own. How then can he value someone else's? But to the person to whom his own faith is precious, so too are others. Because he cherishes his own, he values someone else's. His may be diamonds, the other emeralds, •

but he sees the beauty in each. So, the Rebbe ended, in most cases if not all you will find that your attachment to Judaism will heighten your appreciation of the gifts of other cultures. In other words, the more deeply you value what is yours, the more you will value the achievements of others.

This was a marvelous reply. More important, it was true, as I discovered many times as the years passed. I found that those who are most at ease in their own faith have a capacity to recognize moral and spiritual greatness in whatever form it takes. Secure in their identity, confident in their beliefs, they have an openness and generosity that allows them to respond to other people and other languages of the spirit.

The third moment took place when I had finished university and was teaching philosophy. At that time, most of my other colleagues were Marxists. Some were Jewish, most not, but almost all were irreligious or antireligious. In those days I had no thought of eventually becoming a rabbi, but the lesson of my childhood had stayed with me enough to make me wear my *yarmulka* at all times. One particularly windy day, as I was crossing the playing fields, it blew off and instead of putting it back, I carried it until I reached the lecture room.

The next day I was summoned by the head of the department. "Is everything all right, Jonathan?" he asked. "Yes," I replied, puzzled by his question. "It's just that I saw you yesterday crossing the playing field not wearing your skullcap, and I wondered whether anything had happened." It was an astonishing moment. I suddenly realized that though he was not Jewish, he was deeply troubled at the thought that I might be losing my faith—whether out of philosophical doubt or the sheer isolation of being the only religious Jew on campus. I don't know if even now I fully understand his reaction, but I think it meant that my being true to my faith was part of the security of his world. Knowing where I was, he knew where he was. He was neither religious nor Jewish, but in some obscure way it helped him to know that there were people who were both, and if I gave up, something larger was giving way.

Since then I have encountered this phenomenon so many times in different ways that I am tempted to assert it in the form of two principles which, if not always true, are true more often than not: Non-Jews respect Jews who respect Judaism, and they are embarrassed by Jews who are embarrassed by Judaism.

Ambivalence is bad for us, for those who relate to us, and above all for our children. And ambivalence has been writ large in the identity of Jews for the last two centuries. An entire literature, Jewish and non-Jewish, testifies to it. Perhaps it was inevitable, given the double-bind of emancipation. Jews, embarrassed to be Jews, resolved the tension by keeping the lowest possible profile. As Sidney Morganbesser wittily put it, the Jewish maxim was *Incognito, ergo sum*, "I am invisible, therefore I am."[5]

Ambivalence spells the end of an identity because it cannot be passed on to our children. They will seek, for their own psychic health, to escape from it; and that in effect is what a whole generation is doing by leaving Judaism. It is a tragedy, and not only for ourselves. For as long as Jews are Jews, they contribute something unique to the intellectual, spiritual and moral life of society. So that if Jews are no longer Jews, there is a missing voice, an empty place, in the conversation of mankind. It is only by being what we uniquely are that we contribute what we alone can give. It is precisely by being different, singular, in-but-not-altogether-of this time and place that Jews have so often been a distinctive voice in the Western story of the spirit and the mind.

I believe that a terrible fallacy was born in the minds of the Jews of the nineteenth century, one that has wreaked havoc with Jewry ever since. The fallacy was that Jews are the cause of anti-Semitism. Therefore if Jews change, anti-Semitism will disappear. This is false simply because Jews are the object rather than the cause of anti-Semitism, and this is something else altogether—not less fearful, nor less tragic in its consequences, but different.

One of the best-known facts about anti-Semitism is that its existence does not require the presence of Jews. It exists in countries that do not have, perhaps never had, a significant Jewish population. Jews can fight anti-Semitism, but they cannot cure it. Only anti-Semites can do that. That is what the Church has been attempting to do, often with great courage, since the Holocaust. It is what Germany has tried to do in its own wrestling match of the soul. Tragically, of course, anti-Semitism has not died. It has merely traveled, and today it exists in the form of an Islamic anti-Zionism no less demonic than its Christian antecedents.

The only sane response to anti-Semitism is to monitor it, fight it, but never let it affect our idea of who we are. Pride is always a healthier response than shame. Some years ago a rabbi told me of an episode that happened to him in Russia. *Glasnost* was in its early days. For the first time in seventy years, Jews were free to practice Judaism openly. He had gone there to help in the revival of Jewish life. He discovered, as many did at that time, that "openness" meant also that anti-Semitism could be more freely expressed.

One day a young woman came to him in distress. All her

life, she said, she had hidden the fact that she was a Jew, and she still did. Now, though, for the first time, her neighbors muttered *Zhid* ("Jew") when she passed. What could she do? The rabbi thought, then said this. "If you had not come to me with your story I would have no way of knowing that you are a Jew. But when I walk in the street, people can see I am a Jew. I wear a *yarmulka*. I look like a rabbi. Yet in all the months I have been here, no one has said to me *Zhid*. Why do you think that is?" The girl took a minute to reflect, then said, "Because they know that if they call me 'Jew' I will take it as an insult. But if they call you 'Jew' you will take it as a compliment."

There is all the difference in the world between pride and arrogance. Arrogance is the belief that you are better than others. Jews have sometimes been guilty of this, and it is inexcusable. Pride is simply knowing that each of us is different and being at ease with that fact, never "desiring this man's gift and that man's scope."[6] Arrogance diminishes others, and therefore diminishes us. Pride values others, because we have learned to value ourselves.

I learned this lesson from an old Israeli boatman in Eilat. We had gone there, my wife and I, to find the sun after a cold northern winter. Eilat is hot but bleak, set in the desert among brown and barren hills. There is not much to do there, so one morning we decided to go out in one of the glass-bottomed boats, through which you can see the multicolored fish that swim in Eilat's waters. We were the only passengers on that trip.

The captain overheard us talking and rushed over to us. *Atem me-Anglia?* "Are you from England?" Yes, we said. Why did he want to know? Ah, he said, I have just come back from a holiday there. What did he think of England? "Wonderful! The grass—so green! The buildings—so old! The people—so polite!" And then a vast smile filled his face, and he spread his arms and looked around him at the barren desert hills and said, with an air of infinite delight, *Aval zeh shelanu*, "But this is ours."

Then I knew what it is to be a Jew. There are other cultures, other civilizations, other peoples, other faiths. Each has contributed something unique to the total experience of mankind. Each, from its own vantage point, has been chosen. *But this is ours.* This is our faith, our people, our heritage. By loving them, I learn to love humanity in its diversity. At peace with myself, I find peace with the world.

16

Why I Am a Jew

"SOME PEOPLE LIKE THE JEWS, AND SOME DO NOT," said Winston Churchill. "But no thoughtful man can deny the fact that they are beyond question the most formidable and the most remarkable race which has ever appeared in the world."[1] I have tried to say what it means to me to be part of that people. Jewry survived while every empire that sought its destruction has ceased to be. In our own time, it has passed through the worst crime of man against man, the Holocaust, and yet still it affirms life. Today the Jewish people are not old. If anything they are young. The State of Israel in a mere half century has achieved things for which there is no comparison in any of the hundred or more new states that have come into being in the United Nations since the end of the Second World War. To be part of that history is a rare and precious heritage, and one of which I am proud.

Albert Einstein once said, "The pursuit of knowledge for its own sake, an almost fanatical love of justice and the desire for personal independence—these are the features of the Jewish tradition which make me thank my stars I belong to it."[2] I share his sense of gratitude. It is more than thirty years since I began my own personal journey toward faith, and time and again I have been enthralled by the discoveries I have made along the way. Judaism is an adult faith. It does not call for the suspension of disbelief or what *Alice in Wonderland*'s Queen described as "believing six impossible things before breakfast."[3] Surely no religion has more actively encouraged the asking of questions, above all within the *yeshivah*, the citadel of traditional Jewish learning. Rabbi Abraham Twerski describes a moment familiar to anyone who has spent time in such an environment. When he was young, his instructor would relish challenges to his arguments, the more forceful the better. In his broken English he would say, "You right! You a hundred prozent right! Now I show you where you wrong."[4] And there is a moving honesty about the Jewish mind. Despite the formidable intellectual energies Jews have devoted throughout the centuries to interpreting the will and word of God, they rarely wrote systematic theologies. They prayed to God and argued with Him, but they did not try to fit Him into the finite categories of human thought. They never forgot that God is more like a person than a concept, and therefore there will always be much about Him that eludes understanding.

And then there is the immense moral energy at the core of Jewish life, that "almost fanatical love of justice" that connects Abraham and Moses with the Jewish civil rights and anti-apartheid activists of more recent times. I have tried, in this book, to trace it back to the haunting image of the palace in flames, and to the tension between the world as it is and as it ought to be, that only action can resolve. The late Rabbi Joseph Soloveitchik, one of the outstanding Orthodox thinkers of the twentieth century, recounts an occasion when his grandfather, Rabbi Hayyim of Brisk, was asked what the function of a rabbi is. Without hesitation he replied, "To redress the grievances of those who are abandoned and alone, to protect the dignity of the poor, and to save the oppressed from the hands of his oppressor."[5] Why is it that this answer does not surprise us, yet coming from an Oxford or Harvard professor it might? "Reb Hayyim," as he was known, was one of the legendary scholars of the Volozhyn *yeshivah* in the nineteenth century, and yet Judaism's houses of study were rarely detached from social concern for the community as a whole. It was well known that Reb Hayyim would give away most of his salary to the poor and leave his wood store unlocked so that anyone needing fuel could come and take it. When his layleaders complained about the cost, he replied that in that case he would have to instruct his wife never to light the fire because he could not sit in the warmth while the poor went cold.[6] There is a direct line between Reb Hayyim and the 50 percent of California Jews who, when asked what being Jewish meant to them, replied "social justice"—three times the figure for any other factor.[7] The restless drive to "perfect the world under the sovereignty of God" is a Jewish instinct that survives long after other practices have been abandoned.

Was it the insistence on the absolute transcendence of God that allowed Jews to see the human situation so clearly, understanding both our smallness and potential greatness as "partners with the Holy One, blessed be He, in the work of creation"? Unlike Christianity, Judaism is not a religion of salvation. We do not believe that we stand under the shadow of "original sin" and therefore need to be saved. Nor, like so many secular systems from ancient Greece to today, do we see the individual as fundamentally alone in a sea of hostile, or at best indifferent, forces. It is not that these are untenable views; they have given rise to major civilizations. Yet it would be hard to find another people who, over time, have endowed the human individual with more dignity and responsibility. Perhaps that is why, although Jewry has always been small—today, a mere quarter of a percent of the population of the world—its impact has been so disproportionate to its numbers. Judaism expects great things of its adherents; a people who saw themselves as a "kingdom of priests" could do no less. And high expectations give rise to high achievements.

I once asked Paul Johnson, the Catholic writer from whose *A History of the Jews* I have quoted more than once, what he most admired about Judaism. He replied that no other faith or culture had managed so well the balance between individual and collective responsibility, summarized in Hillel's famous aphorism, "If I am not for myself, who will be? And if I am only for myself, what am I?"[8] It was, he said, an extraordinarily difficult balance to achieve; most other cultures had slid, at some time or other, into excessive individualism or oppressive collectivism. It was a wise observation, and as I have reflected on it over the years it seems to me that Judaism, from its earliest days, understood the way character is formed, as a series of outward movements from family to community to people to humanity as a whole. We were blessed by not having the overly abstract imagination of the Greeks. Jews did not think in terms of disembodied categories like "the individual" and "the collective." We are both. We grow as individuals through our moral connectedness to others, and surely no religion has endowed the vehicles of that connectedness—the home, the school, the congregation, the sense of kinship with a people scattered through time and space—with a more carefully orchestrated beauty. We are a people of strong individuals; no one who has attended a Jewish committee meeting could believe otherwise. And yet even the most unaffiliated Jew feels a strong sense of responsibility to others, as one sees whenever Israel or some other Jewish community is under threat.

I believe that Judaism got it right about the big questions: God and mankind, the universal and the particular, the individual and society, education and the life of the mind, justice and compassion, human dignity and equality, being part of yet apart from the wider society in which we are set. I am not a social Darwinian, yet I believe that Jews and Judaism would not have survived for so long, under such varied and often adverse conditions, without having discovered some profound set of truths about the human condition. From the earliest days, with no obvious facts to support them, our ancestors were convinced that the vision by which they felt themselves addressed would endure as long as man walked the earth; and thus far they have been proved correct. The covenantal drama, for all its improbability, has unfolded more or less as they said it would. If this is not a proof, then at least it is an intimation, that Jewish history has been a scroll through which God, in distinctive handwriting, has sent a message to mankind.

I cannot hide my sense that something is wrong with Jewish life today. I see it in almost every direction I look. It is not only that young Jews are disengaging from Judaism at a rate virtually unprecedented in history. Nor is it the grievous and unnecessary fractiousness that injures the relationships between the various Jewish groups, religious and secular,

Orthodox and liberal, and the different strands within Orthodoxy itself. It is, rather, an inescapable feeling that we have somehow lost the script of the Jewish story, that breathtaking attempt to build, out of simple acts and ordinary lives, a fragment of heaven on earth, a society of human dignity under the sovereignty of God, a home for the Divine presence.

Never in the past two thousand years have the opportunities been greater or the stakes so high. In Israel, for the first time since the days of the Romans, Jews have the chance to build a society and culture along Jewish lines. The Jewish people has its own nation-state, set in the landscape of the prophets, resonating to the language of the Bible and surrounded by visible reminders of its history. In most countries of the Diaspora, Jews have won more than equality and civil rights; they are among its most highly achieving groups. Besides this, and partly as a result of the impact of the Holocaust on the West, most liberal democracies today are self-consciously pluralist, multiethnic and religiously diverse. That does not mean that anti-Semitism no longer exists; it does. But neither now nor in the foreseeable future can it hold center stage in the political arena. The days when *die Judenfrage,* "the Jewish question," dominated dinner-table conversations in Europe are gone.

Times without number I have been surprised by the admiration non-Jews have for Jewish life. Perhaps, as a Chief Rabbi, I have had unusual opportunities to see this at first hand. I have studied Torah with the future king of England and with its present prime minister. I have had close relationships with archbishops and cardinals, and been approached for guidance by non-Jewish groups throughout the world, from labor organizers in the United States to mineworkers in South Africa to government ministers and leaders of the

British armed forces. These have all been people who have had no special reason to be interested in Judaism, yet they are. They see it as a source of wisdom and as a set of institutions of compelling strength. They respect the closeness of a Jewish family, the warmth of the Jewish home, our passion for education, our commitment to *tzedakah*, giving to others. They are aware of the Jewish contribution to almost every aspect of modern culture and are fascinated by that awe-inspiring capacity to retain a sense of humor in the midst, and without diminishing the depth, of Jewish suffering. They cannot understand why Jews would wish to relinquish this heritage. Neither can I, which is why I have written this book.

Perhaps in the end it comes down to faith. Jews were and are a people whose identity makes sense, in the long run, only in religious terms, albeit terms which are unique among the religions of the world. We are not, nor can we predicate our survival on remaining, an ethnic group, a secular culture, or a constellation of fading memories, a benign but undemanding nostalgia. Each of these can provide the basis of an identity, but it is one that has a life span of at most three generations, and already most of our children are four generations removed from the *shtetl*, the *heim* and the world of "tradition." Ethnicity carries no obligations. Culture does not command. Memory, in and of itself, does not ask of us that we commit ourselves to perpetuating what it is we remember. That is why groups built on these foundations inevitably disappear over time.

Judaism was always larger than this, one of the noblest dreams ever to take hold of the human imagination—the idea that God, in His lonely singularity, might reach out to an individual, then to a nation, in its lonely singularity, proposing a partnership whereby, deed by deed and generation by generation, together they might fashion a living example of what it is to honor the humanity of God and the image of God that is the human person. And as long as Jews were Jews, living by the word of God, a light did radiate in their collective lives, the light we call the *Shekhinah*, the Divine indwelling presence, that bathes a Shabbat table or a family conversation with its beauty and a sense of eternity in the here-and-now.

Can we ever really know whether faith is justified? Do we, citizens of modernity and post-modernity, not take for granted what Hume, Kant and Nietzsche labored to establish, that the existence of God cannot be proved? And do we not as Jews—always inclined to rationality, and now chastened and chilled by the Holocaust—have more reason to doubt than most? Yet I have to admit, even as a professionally trained philosopher, that I am unmoved by this whole trend of thought, rendered trivial by its own circularity. Of course it is possible to live a life without God, just as it is possible to live a life without humor, or music, or love; and one can no more prove that God exists than one can prove these other things exist to those who lack a sense of humor, or to whom Schubert is mere noise, or love a figment of the romantic imagination. The late Sir Isaiah Berlin used to say to me, in his sonorous voice and with a mischievous smile, "Chief Rabbi, don't talk to me about faith. When it comes to God, I'm *tone-deaf*." I never argued the point with him: at the age of eighty, I felt he was entitled to his agnosticism. But on reflection I see I should have done so. He had striven to appreciate music and poetry, Russian literature and the history of ideas. He knew that one can live a life without these things, but it will be a smaller, more circumscribed and impoverished life. How much more so in the case of faith.

Jewish faith is not a metaphysical wager, a leap into the

improbable. It is the courage to see the world as it is, without the comfort of myth or the self-pity of despair, knowing that the evil, cruelty and injustice it contains are neither inevitable nor meaningless but instead a call to human responsibility—a call emanating from the heart of existence itself. The political commentator William Safire comes to a powerful conclusion at the end of his study of the Book of Job. It is a book, he writes, with no easy answers. Yet it remains "the greatest form of solace and source of strength," because its message is that "No matter how solitary the confinement, the individual human being is not alone in the universe."[9] Jewish faith is false only if we are wrong to believe in the objective reality of all that is personal. No religion has given God a more human face, or humanity a more awesome challenge, or history a more hope-laden script. None has more deeply challenged us, its guardians, to grow; and none has paid greater respect to critical intelligence and human responsibility.

I believe that at a certain point in history—it happened at different times in different countries—Jews lost their faith in God and placed their trust in man. That, of course, has been the story of Western civilization as a whole, but it happened to Jews more suddenly and poignantly than to anyone else. They had suffered long and hard for their convictions. Lacking power for centuries, they had begun to see religious faith as passive, a reliance of man on God, rather than what it was for the patriarchs and prophets, the call of God to man. Now, beginning with the French Revolution, a new secular dispensation seemed to answer their prayers, and they invested it with all the hopes of a profoundly religious people. Alasdair MacIntyre once pointed out that there are two types of atheist, one who simply does not believe, and one who disbelieves with an almost religious fervor.[10] Of the latter kind, a disproportionate number—they include Spinoza, Marx and Freud—have been Jews.

It turned out to be the wrong choice. Jews found themselves caught between the lure of Emancipation and the double bind of anti-Semitism, and out of that vortex came both the nightmare and the dream of modern Jewish life: the Holocaust and the birth of the State of Israel. The outward story of those years is engraved in every Jewish mind, but the inner story is more tempestuous and not yet resolved. When Jews began to define themselves horizontally, in terms of their relationship to those around them, they found themselves prey to a range of syndromes from insecurity to aggression, from self-hatred to a narrow ethnic pride. Collective traumas of this magnitude take several generations to play themselves out, and we still live with their aftershocks. Like Jacob after his wrestling match with the angel, we limp.

Jewish identity, I believe, can never be merely horizontal, synchronic, secular, untouched by the still, small voice of eternity and destiny. We are a vertical people, linked through a covenantal bond to the past, the future, and to heaven itself. G. K. Chesterton once said that the United States was the only nation ever to be built on a creed.[11] He was wrong: the Jewish people were conceived and born on the basis of a belief, articulated at Mount Sinai, made explicit in the Torah, and realized in more than a hundred generations of individual lives. Take that away, and Jewish identity loses its coherence as surely as would the United States if Americans forgot the phrase "life, liberty and the pursuit of happiness." To be a Jew is to be part of the ongoing dialogue between earth and heaven that has persisted for two thirds of the recorded history of civilization and whose theme is as urgent now as at any time in the past: to build a society that honors the human person in our differences and commonalities, our singularity and interdependence. Rarely have we needed it more than in our present age of Promethean technological powers, and seldom has its power been more evident than now as, throughout the West, families, communities, the moral sense itself, have come under assault.

Above all—and this has been my central theme—Judaism is not a theory, a system, a set of speculative propositions, an "ism." It is a call, and it bears our name. Unlike the other great monotheisms, Christianity and Islam, and equally unlike the philosophies of the Greeks and their successors, Judaism is not a truth addressed to all mankind. It is a summons to us, mediated through more than a hundred generations of our ancestors, written in the history of their lives and now confronting us as our heritage and responsibility. One of the most profound religious truths Judaism ever articulated was that God loves diversity; He does not ask us all to serve Him in the same way. To each people He has set a challenge, and with the Jewish people He made a covenant, knowing that it takes time, centuries, millennia, to overcome the conflicts and injustices of the human situation, and that therefore each generation must hand on its ideals to the next, so that there will always be a Jewish people conveying its particular vision to humanity and moving, however haltingly, to a more gracious world. The most eloquent words God spoke to Abraham, Jacob, Moses and the prophets was to call their name. Their reply was simply *Hineni*, "Here I am." That is the call Jewish history makes to us: to continue the story and to write our letter in the scroll.

· · ·

Why, then, am I a Jew? Not because I believe that Judaism
contains all there is of the human story. Jews didn't write
Shakespeare's sonnets or Beethoven's quartets. We did not
give the world the serene beauty of a Japanese garden or the
architecture of ancient Greece. I love these things. I admire
the traditions that brought them forth. *Aval zeh shelanu*. But
this is ours. Nor am I a Jew because of anti-Semitism or to
avoid giving Hitler a posthumous victory. What happens to
me does not define who I am: ours is a people of faith, not
fate. Nor is it because I think that Jews are better than others,
more intelligent, virtuous, law-abiding, creative, generous or
successful. The difference lies not in Jews but Judaism, not in
what we are but in what we are called on to be.

I am a Jew because, being a child of my people, I have
heard the call to add my chapter to its unfinished story. I am
a stage on its journey, a connecting link between the generations. The dreams and hopes of my ancestors live on in
me, and I am the guardian of their trust, now and for the future.

I am a Jew because our ancestors were the first to see that
the world is driven by a moral purpose, that reality is not a
ceaseless war of the elements, to be worshiped as gods, nor
history a battle in which might is right and power is to be
appeased. The Judaic tradition shaped the moral civilization of the West, teaching for the first time that human life
is sacred, that the individual may never be sacrificed for the
mass, and that rich and poor, great and small, are all equal
before God.

I am a Jew because I am the moral heir of those who
stood at the foot of Mount Sinai and pledged themselves to
live by these truths, becoming a kingdom of priests and a
holy nation. I am the descendant of countless generations of
ancestors who, though sorely tested and bitterly tried, re-

mained faithful to that covenant when they might so easily have defected.

I am a Jew because of Shabbat, the world's greatest religious institution, a time in which there is no manipulation of nature or our fellow human beings, in which we come together in freedom and equality to create, every week, an anticipation of the messianic age.

I am a Jew because our nation, though at times it suffered the deepest poverty, never gave up on its commitment to helping the poor, or rescuing Jews from other lands, or fighting for justice for the oppressed, and did so without self-congratulation, because it was a *mitzvah*, because a Jew could do no less.

I am a Jew because I cherish the Torah, knowing that God is to be found not in natural forces but in moral meanings, in words, texts, teachings and commands, and because Jews, though they lacked all else, never ceased to value education as a sacred task, endowing the individual with dignity and depth.

I am a Jew because of our people's passionate faith in freedom, holding that each of us is a moral agent, and that in this lies our unique dignity as human beings; and because Judaism never left its ideals at the level of lofty aspirations, but instead translated them into deeds that we call *mitzvot*, and a way, which we call the *halakhah*, and thus brought heaven down to earth.

I am proud, simply, to be a Jew.

I am proud to be part of a people who, though scarred and traumatized, never lost their humor or their faith, their ability to laugh at present troubles and still believe in ultimate redemption; who saw human history as a journey, and never stopped traveling and searching.

I am proud to be part of an age in which my people, ravaged by the worst crime ever to be committed against a people, responded by reviving a land, recovering their sovereignty, rescuing threatened Jews throughout the world, rebuilding Jerusalem, and proving themselves to be as courageous in the pursuit of peace as in defending themselves in war.

I am proud that our ancestors refused to be satisfied with premature consolations, and in answer to the question, "Has the Messiah come?" always answered, "Not yet."

I am proud to belong to the people Israel, whose name means "one who wrestles with God and with man and prevails." For though we have loved humanity, we have never stopped wrestling with it, challenging the idols of every age. And though we have loved God with an everlasting love, we have never stopped wrestling with Him nor He with us.

And though I admire other civilizations and faiths, and believe each has brought something special into the world, still this is my people, my heritage, my God. In our uniqueness lies our universality. Through being what we alone are, we give to humanity what only we can give.

This, then, is our story, our gift to the next generation. I received it from my parents and they from theirs across great expanses of space and time. There is nothing quite like it. It changed and today it still challenges the moral imagination of mankind. I want to say to my children: Take it, cherish it, learn to understand and to love it. Carry it, and it will carry you. And may you in turn pass it on to your children. For you are a member of an eternal people, a letter in their scroll. Let their eternity live on in you.

Notes

All biblical and rabbinic translations are my own, unless otherwise indicated.

PROLOGUE

1. Quoted in J. H. Hertz, *A Book of Jewish Thoughts*, Oxford University Press, London, 1926, 135.
2. John Adams to F. A. Vanderkemp, February 16, 1809, in *The Works of John Adams*, ed. C. F. Adams, vol. 9, pp. 609–10.
3. Paul Johnson, *A History of the Jews*, Weidenfeld & Nicolson, London, 1987, 585.
4. William Rees Mogg, *The Reigning Error*, Hamish Hamilton, London, 1974, 11.
5. Milton Himmelfarb, *The Jews of Modernity*, Basic Books, New York, 1973, 359.
6. Edmond Fleg, *Why I Am a Jew*, trans. Victor Gollancz, Gollancz, London, 1943.
7. Deuteronomy 6:7.
8. Deuteronomy 6:5.
9. Moses Alshekh, *Torat Mosheh* to Deuteronomy 6:6.
10. Wordsworth, *The Prelude*, book 14, 1. 446–47.

Chapter 1: Why Be Jewish?

1. Deuteronomy 29:9–14. *New International Version* translation.
2. Isaac Arama, *Akedat Yitzhak*, Gate 99. In the standard edition of this work, reprinted many times, the discussion can be found in vol. 5, 103b–109a.
3. Rashi to Deuteronomy 29:14.
4. Babylonian Talmud, *Yoma* 73b, *Nedarim* 8a, *Shevuot* 21b, 22b, 25a.
5. Babylonian Talmud, *Baba Metzia* 12a, *Hullin* 83a.
6. *Midrash Shir ha-Shirim Rabbah*, I, 4, 1.
7. Judah Halevi, *Kuzari*, Book I, para. 115.
8. A full translation can be found in Abraham Halkin and David Hartman, *Crisis and Leadership: Epistles of Maimonides*, Jewish Publication Society of America, Philadelphia, 1985, 93–149.
9. Ibid. 102–103.
10. Abrabanel, *Zevah Pesah*, Constantinople, 1505, fol. 35r.
11. Ezekiel 20:32.
12. Babylonian Talmud, *Baba Batra*, 60b.
13. Babylonian Talmud, *Sanhedrin* 105a.
14. Elie Wiesel, "Jewish Values in the Post-Holocaust Future," *Judaism*, Summer 1967, Volume 16:3, 281.

Chapter 2: Answers

1. Arama, *Akedat Yitzhak* to Deuteronomy 29:10, Volume 5, 108a.
2. Abrabanel, *Commentary* to Deuteronomy 29:10.
3. Ezekiel 20:32–33.
4. Quoted in Haim Beinart, *Conversos on Trial: The Inquisition in Ciudad Real*, Magnes Press, Hebrew University, Jerusalem, 1981, 3.
5. Abrabanel, *Commentary* to Ezekiel 20:32.
6. See Elie Kedourie (ed.), *Spain and the Jews: The Sephardi Experience 1492 and After*, Thames & Hudson, London, 1992.
7. Moses Hess, *Rome and Jerusalem*, trans. Maurice J. Bloom, Philosophical Library, New York, 1958, 25.

8. It has been estimated that, at the time of the destruction of the second Temple in the first century C.E., Jews numbered some 8 million people, approximately 10 percent of the population of the Roman Empire (*Enyclopaedia Judaica*, xiii, 871). In 1995 the world Jewish population was estimated to be 12.8 million out of a world population of 5.8 billion, or less than one-quarter of a percent (cited in Michael Novak, *Tell Me Why*, Lion Publishing, Oxford, 1999, 91).

9. Babylonian Talmud, *Shabbat* 88a.

10. Ibid.

CHAPTER 3: WHO AM I? WHO ARE WE?

1. A. J. Ayer, *Language, Truth and Logic*, Dover, New York, n.d., 102–119.

2. E. R. Leach, *A Runaway World?*, British Broadcasting Corporation, London, 1968, 44.

3. *Mekhilta de-Rabbi Shimon bar Yochai* to Exodus 19:6; ed. by J. N. Epstein and E. Z. Melamed, Jerusalem, n.d., 139.

4. Babylonian Talmud *Sanhedrin* 27b, *Shevuot* 39a.

5. Exodus 12:26–27.

6. Exodus 13:8.

7. Exodus 13:14.

8. Pascal, *Pensées*, trans. A. J. Krailsheimer, Penguin, Harmondsworth, 1968, 171, 176–77.

9. Quoted in Hertz, *A Book of Jewish Thoughts*, 136.

10. Quoted in Isadore Twersky, "Survival, Normalcy, Modernity," in *Zionism in Transition*, Moshe Davis (ed.), Arno Press, New York, 1980, 349.

CHAPTER 4: A LETTER IN THE SCROLL

1. See George Steiner, "Our Homeland, the Text," *Salmagundi*, Winter–Spring 1985, 4–25. The early rabbinic literature contained a similar thought: "Even though they are exiled, when Jews engage in Torah, they are at home." *Seder*

Eliyyahu Rabbah, ed. Meir Friedmann, Vienna, 1902, chapter 28, 148.

2. Thomas Cahill, *The Gifts of the Jews*, Doubleday, New York, 1998.

3. A. L. Rowse, *Historians I Have Known*, Duckworth, London, 1995.

CHAPTER 5: A PALACE IN FLAMES

1. Genesis 12:2–3.

2. Genesis 18:19.

3. *Midrash Bereshit Rabbah*, 42:8.

4. Deuteronomy 7:7.

5. See Isaiah 43:10.

6. Babylonian Talmud, *Shabbat* 10a, 119b, *Sanhedrin* 38a.

7. Paul Johnson, *A History of the Jews*, Weidenfeld & Nicolson, London, 1987, 2.

8. *Seder Eliyyahu Rabbah*, ed. Meir Friedmann, Vilna, 1902, 27–28; *Midrash Bereshit Rabbah*, 38:13; Hayim Nahman Bialik and Yehoshua Ravnitzky, *The Book of Legends*, translated by William G. Braude, Schocken Books, New York, 1992, 32–3.

9. Maimonides, *Mishneh Torah*, Laws of Idolatry, 1:2–3.

10. *Midrash Bereshit Rabbah*, 39:1.

11. A. J. Heschel, *God in Search of Man: A Philosophy of Judaism*, John Calder, London, 1956, 112.

12. Louis Jacobs, *We Have Reason to Believe*, Vallentine Mitchell, London, 1957, 23. But see also Louis Jacobs, *Principles of the Jewish Faith*, Vallentine Mitchell, London, 1964, 43, where the author correctly interprets the passage as a statement, not of the argument from design but of the problem of evil.

13. The phrase is derived from the words of the *Alenu* prayer, *le-takken olam be-malkhut Shaddai*, "to perfect the world under the sovereignty of the Almighty." For the development of the idea in Lurianic kabbalah, see Gershom Scholem, *Major Trends in Jewish Mysticism*, Thames & Hudson, London, 1955, 244–86.

CHAPTER 6: THE IDEA OF MAN

1. Cahill, *The Gifts of the Jews*, 240–41.
2. See Karen Armstrong, *A History of God*, Mandarin, London, 1993, 9–50.
3. Genesis 1:27.
4. Lionel Trilling, *Sincerity and Authenticity*, Harvard University Press, Cambridge, 1972, 24.
5. Max Weber, *Ancient Judaism*, The Free Press, New York, 1952. See also Peter Berger, *The Sacred Canopy*, Doubleday, New York, 1967; Irving M. Zeitlin, *Ancient Judaism*, Polity Press, Cambridge, 1984, 1–35.
6. In Erich Auerbach, *Mimesis*, trans. Willard R. Trask, Princeton University Press, Princeton, N.J., 1971, 3–23.
7. Genesis 9:6.

CHAPTER 7: COVENANTAL MORALITY

1. Genesis 2:18.
2. See Jack Miles, *God: A Biography*, Simon & Schuster, London, 1995.
3. Psalm 8:5–6.
4. Genesis 2:23.
5. Genesis 19:5.
6. See Rashi to Genesis 2:18.
7. Genesis 3:20.
8. On trust as the basis of social interaction, see Francis Fukuyama, *Trust: The Social Virtues and the Creation of Prosperity*, The Free Press, New York, 1995.
9. See J. L. Austin, *How to Do Things with Words*, ed. J. O. Urmson, Clarendon Press, Oxford, 1975; John R. Searle, *Speech Acts: An Essay in the Philosophy of Language*, Cambridge University Press, London, 1969.
10. Hosea 2:21–2.
11. See Menachem Kellner, *Must a Jew Believe Anything?*, Littman Library, London, 1999, 11–25.
12. Hosea 2:18.
13. I Kings 19:11–13.
14. Genesis 12:3.

CHAPTER 8: THE CHOSEN PEOPLE

1. Isaiah Berlin, "Two Concepts of Liberty," in *Four Essays on Liberty*, Oxford University Press, Oxford, 1969, 167.
2. Genesis 6:11.
3. See Michael Wyschogrod, *The Body of Faith: Judaism as Corporeal Election*, Seabury Press, Minneapolis, 1983, esp. 58–65.
4. Exodus 3:14.
5. Deuteronomy 23:8.
6. See R. J. Zwi Werblowski, *Between Tradition and Modernity*, Athlone Press, London, 40–42.
7. Babylonian Talmud, *Sanhedrin* 39b.
8. Leviticus 19:17.
9. Exodus 23:9.
10. Leviticus 19:33–34.
11. Babylonian Talmud, *Baba Metzia* 59b.
12. Genesis 23:4.
13. Exodus 18:3.
14. Micah 4:3–5.
15. I Chronicles 22:8.
16. Traditional.
17. Lewis Browne (ed.), *The Wisdom of Israel*, Michael Joseph, London, 1949, 578–9.
18. Genesis 6:9.
19. Genesis 6:22; 7:5, 9, 16.
20. Genesis 18:23–25.
21. Babylonian Talmud, *Sanhedrin* 105a.
22. See Anson Laytner, *Arguing with God: A Jewish Tradition*, Jason Aronson, Northvale, N.J., 1990.
23. Babylonian Talmud, *Berakhot* 60b.
24. C. S. Lewis, *The Abolition of Man*, Oxford University Press, Oxford, 1943.

CHAPTER 9: EXODUS AND REVELATION

1. Nelson Mandela, *Long Walk to Freedom*, Little Brown, London, 1994.

2. Mishnah, *Pesahim* 10:5: "In every generation, a person is obligated to see himself as if he personally had left Egypt."

3. Yosef Hayim Yerushalmi, *Zakhor: Jewish History and Jewish Memory,* Schocken Books, New York, 1989, 9: "Only in Israel and nowhere else is the injunction to remember felt as a religious imperative to an entire people."

4. Genesis 15:2.

5. Genesis 22:2.

6. Genesis 22:12.

7. John Stuart Mill, *Essays on Politics and Culture,* ed. Gertrude Himmelfarb, Garden City, New York, Doubleday, 1962, 137: "Whenever and in proportion as the strictness of the restraining discipline was relaxed, the natural tendency of mankind to anarchy reasserted itself; the state became disorganized from within; mutual conflict for selfish ends neutralized the energies which were required to keep up the contest against natural causes of evil; and the nation, after a longer or briefer interval of progressive decline, became either the slave of a despotism or the prey of a foreign invader."

8. Deuteronomy 26:5.

9. Exodus 19:4–6.

10. On this distinction see Rabbi Joseph B. Soloveitchik, "Kol Dodi Dofek: It is the voice of my beloved that knocketh," trans. Lawrence Kaplan, in *Theological and Halakhic Reflections on the Holocaust,* Bernhard H. Rosenberg (ed.), Ktav, New York, 1992, 51–117.

11. Daniel Elazar, *People and Polity,* Detroit, Wayne State University Press, 1989, 23.

12. Exodus 1:9.

13. Genesis 43:32.

14. See Delbert Hillers, *Covenant: The History of a Biblical Idea,* Johns Hopkins University Press, Baltimore, 1969; George E. Mendenhall, *Law and Covenant in Israel and the Ancient Near East,* The Biblical Colloquium, Pittsburgh, 1955; John Bright, *Covenant and Promise: The Prophetic Understanding of the Future in Pre-Exilic Israel,* Westminster Press, Philadelphia, 1976.

15. Exodus 19:8.

16. Alexis de Tocqueville, *Democracy in America*, abridged with an introduction by Thomas Bender, Modern Library, New York, 1981, 145–158; John Stuart Mill, *Utilitarianism, On Liberty and Considerations on Representative Government*, ed. H. B. Acton, Dent, Everyman's Library, London, 1984, 73.
17. Genesis 14:18.
18. Genesis 47:22.
19. "Two Concepts of Liberty," in Isaiah Berlin, *Four Essays on Liberty*, 118–172.
20. Michael Walzer, *Exodus and Revolution*, Basic Books, New York, 1985, 108–9.

Chapter 10: Covenantal Society

1. Deuteronomy 17:14–20. According to Maimonides, the appointment of a king was obligatory. For Ibn Ezra it was permissible rather than mandatory, and for Abrabanel it was a concession to popular sentiment. For a discussion of these views, see Nehama Leibowitz, *Studies in Devarim*, World Zionist Organisation, Jerusalem, 1980, 175–180.
2. I Samuel 8:1–9.
3. Ibid., v. 18.
4. Judges 17:6, 21:25.
5. Hobbes, *Leviathan*, ed. Richard Tuck, Cambridge University Press, Cambridge, 1991, 89.
6. See Jonathan Sacks *The Politics of Hope*, Jonathan Cape, London, 1997, 55–65; Daniel Elazar, "The Covenant as the Basis of the Jewish Political Tradition," in *Kinship and Consent: The Jewish Political Tradition and its Contemporary Uses*, Daniel Elazar (ed.), Turtledove, Ramat Gan (Israel), 1981, 21–58.
7. Babylonian Talmud, *Shabbat* 31a.
8. See "Wealth and Poverty: A Jewish Analysis," in Jonathan Sacks, *Tradition in an Untraditional Age*, Vallentine Mitchell, London, 1990, 183-202.
9. Micah 4:4.
10. See Jonathan Sacks, *Morals and Markets*, London Institute of Economic Affairs, 1999.
11. Leviticus 25:23.

12. A summary of Jewish laws against needless destruction can be found in *Encyclopaedia Talmudit*, Jerusalem, 1951, vol. 3, 335–7. See also "Jewish Environmental Ethics," in Jonathan Sacks, *Faith in the Future*, Darton, Longman & Todd, London, 1995, 206–213.
13. Genesis 2:15.
14. Thus, for example, in Leviticus 25:25, 35, 39.
15. Exodus 4:22.
16. Genesis 18:19.
17. Deuteronomy 6:7.
18. See Amos Funkenstein and Adin Steinsaltz, *The Sociology of Ignorance* [Hebrew], Galei Zahal, Tel Aviv, 1987.
19. Joseph Naveh, *Early History of the Alphabet*, Magnes Press, Jerusalem, 1987.
20. See Walter J. Ong, *Orality and Literacy*, Routledge, London, 1988.
21. Judges 8:13–14.
22. *Encyclopaedia Britannica*, 15th edition, 1995, vol. 29, 1041.
23. H. G. Wells, *The Outline of History*, George Newnes, London, n.d., 176.
24. Josephus, *Contra Apionem*, ii, 177-8.
25. *Midrash Bereshit Rabbah* 10:9.
26. Ibid.
27. Deuteronomy 5:14–15.
28. This and the next paragraph are adapted from Jonathan Sacks, *The Politics of Hope*, 41–2.
29. Michael Walzer, *Spheres of Justice*, Oxford, Blackwell, 1983, 193.
30. Judah Halevi, *Kuzari*, III, 10.
31. One version of this story is to be found in Martin Buber, *Tales of the Hassidim: Early Masters*, Schocken Books, New York, 1970, 226.
32. Genesis 2:3.

CHAPTER I I: TRAGEDY AND TRIUMPH

1. Babylonian Talmud, *Baba Batra* 60b.
2. Ecclesiastes 7:20.
3. Leviticus 16:2–34.

4. For recent studies, see Hyam Maccoby *The Mythmaker: Paul and the Invention of Christianity*, Harper & Row, New York, 1986; *Paul and Hellenism*, SCM Press, London, 1991; Danial Boyarin, *A Radical Jew: Paul and the Politics of Identity*, University of California Press, Berkeley, 1994; A. N. Wilson *Paul: The Mind of the Apostle*, Norton, New York, 1997.

5. Solomon Schechter, *Aspects of Rabbinic Theology*, Schocken Books, New York, 1961, 242–63; Ephraim E. Urbach, *The Sages: Their Concepts and Beliefs*, Magnes Press, Jerusalem, 1975, 471-83.

6. *Midrash Bereshit Rabbah* 9:7, *Kohelet Rabbah* 3:11.

7. See Louis Finkelstein, *Akiba: Scholar, Saint and Martyr*, Atheneum, New York, 1981.

8. Mishnah, *Yoma* 8:9.

9. Urbach, *The Sages*, 462–471.

10. Micah 6:7–8.

11. Mishnah, *Avot* 3:18.

12. Josephus, *Jewish Antiquities*, 14, 115.

13. The full text of the speech can be found in Victor Gollancz, *A Year of Grace*, Gollancz, London, 1950, 275.

14. See Jules Isaac, *Has Anti-Semitism Roots in Christianity?*, trans. Dorothy and James Parkes, National Conference of Christians and Jews, New York, 1961; Rosemary Radford Ruether *Faith and Fratricide: The Theological Roots of Anti-Semitism*, Seabury Press, New York, 1974; F. E. Talmage *Disputation and Dialogue: Readings in the Jewish-Christian Encounter*, Ktav, New York, 1975.

15. Exodus 2:14.

16. Josephus, *The Jewish War*, trans. G. A. Williamson, Penguin, Harmondsworth, 1959.

17. Mishnah, *Avot* 3:2. Printed editions have "for were it not for the fear of it, men would eat one another alive." See Ephraim Urbach, *The Sages*, 959, note 32.

18. Rabbi Moshe Avigdor Amiel, *Ethics and Legality in Jewish Law*, The Rabbi Amiel Library, Jerusalem, 1992, 70–72.

19. Psalm 137:1–6.

20. Ezekiel 11:16.

21. H. H. Ben-Sasson (ed.), *A History of the Jewish People*, Har-

vard University Press, Cambridge, 1976, 285.

22. See Jonathan Sacks, *Community of Faith*, Peter Halban, London,1995.

23. Salo Wittmayer Baron, *The Jewish Community*, Philadelphia, Jewish Publication Society of America, 1945, vol. 1, 62.

24. Deuteronomy 31:12.

25. "The Covenant as the Basis of the Jewish Political Tradition," in Elazar (ed.), *Kinship and Consent*, 31.

26. Babylonian Talmud, *Sukkah* 51b.

27. Babylonian Talmud, *Pesahim* 101a.

28. Mishnah, *Avot* 1:2.

29. I Kings 8:27.

30. Martin Buber, *Tales of the Hassidim: Later Masters*, Schocken Books, New York, 1948, 277.

CHAPTER 12: TRUTH LIVED

1. Babylonian Talmud, *Gittin* 56b.

2. Babylonian Talmud, *Baba Batra* 21a.

3. Paul Johnson, *A History of the Jews*, 341.

4. Jerusalem Talmud, *Shekalim* 6:1.

5. See Gershom Scholem, *On the Kabbalah and Its Symbolism*, Schocken Books, New York, 1969, 32–86.

6. Babylonian Talmud, *Berakhot* 61b.

7. Babylonian Talmud, *Shabbat* 30a–b.

8. Maimonides, *Mishneh Torah, Laws of Torah Study* 1:6, 10.

9. *Encyclopaedia Judaica*, vol. 6, 407.

10. Baron, *The Jewish Community*, vol. 2, 172.

11. Beryl Smalley, *The Study of the Bible in the Middle Ages*, Blackwell, Oxford, 1952, 78.

12. Maimonides, *Commentary to the Mishnah, Eight Chapters* (prologue to Commentary on Tractate Avot), Introduction. Raymond L. Weiss and Charles Butterworth, *Ethical Writings of Maimonides*, Dover, New York, 1983, 60.

13. Yeshayahu Leibowitz, *Judaism, Human Values and the Jewish State*, ed. Eliezer Goldman, Harvard University Press, Cambridge, 1992, 12–13.

14. Babylonian Talmud, *Horayot*, 13a; Jerusalem Talmud, *Horayot* 3:5.
15. Maimonides, *Mishneh Torah, Laws of Torah Study* 3:1.
16. Psalm 119:45.
17. Mishnah, *Avot* 6:2.
18. See Jonathan Sacks, *Arguments for the Sake of Heaven*, Jason Aronson, Northvale, N. J., 1991, xviii–x.
19. Maimonides, *The Guide of the Perplexed*, III, 31.
20. See Samson Raphael Hirsch, *The Nineteen Letters*, trans. Bernard Drachman, Feldheim, New York, 1969, 78–9.
21. Menachem Kellner, *Dogma in Medieval Jewish Thought*, Oxford University Press, Oxford, 1986.
22. Sacks, *Faith in the Future*, 142–3.
23. Menachem Kellner, *Maimonides on Judaism and the Jewish People*, State University of New York Press, Albany, NY, 1991, 5–7.
24. David Walsh, *Selling Out America's Children*, Fairview Press, Minneapolis, 1995, 3.
25. Bertrand Russell, *History of Western Philosophy*, George Allen & Unwin, London, 1962, 18–19.
26. Quoted in Robert Bellah et al., *Habits of the Heart*, Hutchinson, London, 1988, 294.
27. Matthew Arnold, *Literature and Dogma*, Smith, Elder, London, 1876, 58.

CHAPTER 13: IN THE VALLEY OF THE SHADOW

1. I heard this story from the young man concerned, now Rabbi Yitzhak Rubin of the South Manchester Synagogue.
2. The comment was made in the course of a television documentary series about the world's great religions, *The Long Search*.
3. R. Kalonymous Shapiro, *Eish Kodesh* [no publisher], Jerusalem, 1960, 187. An English version of this work is available: Nehemia Polen, *The Holy Fire: the Teachings of Rabbi Kalonymus Kalman Shapira, the Rebbe of the Warsaw Ghetto*, Jason Aronson, Northvale, N.J., 1994.
4. Job 38:4.
5. Genesis 4:2–10.

6. See *Sifrei* to Deuteronomy 32:4—"'God of faith'—[this means] God had faith in the world and [this is why] He created it."

7. Nietzsche, *Twilight of the Idols and the Anti-Christ*, trans. R. J. Hollingdale, Penguin, Harmondsworth, 1968, 134.

8. Nietzsche, *Beyond Good and Evil*, Penguin, Harmondsworth, 1973, 178.

9. See George Steiner, *In Bluebeard's Castle*, Faber & Faber, London, 1971, 29–48.

10. Genesis 9:6.

11. Song of Songs, 8:6.

12. From the liturgy for the Ninth of Av; Abraham Rosenfeld, *The Authorised Kinot for the Ninth of Av*, Judaica Press, New York, 1983, 216.

13. Psalm 122:3.

CHAPTER 14: AMBIVALENCE AND ASSIMILATION

1. See Voltaire, "Jews," in Paul Mendes-Flohr and Jehuda Reinharz *The Jew in the Modern World*, Oxford University Press, New York, 1980, 252–3.

2. See Anthony Julius, *T. S. Eliot, Anti-Semitism and Literary Form*, Cambridge University Press, Cambridge, 1995, esp. 144–76.

3. Sander L. Gilman, *Jewish Self-Hatred*, Johns Hopkins University Press, Baltimore, 1986.

4. Mordecai Kaplan, *Judaism as a Civilization*, Macmillan, New York, 1934, 3.

5. Amos 3:2.

6. Judah Halevi, *Kuzari*, Book II, para 36.

7. Judah Leib Pinsker, "Auto-Emancipation," in *The Zionist Idea*, ed. Arthur Hertzberg, Atheneum, New York, 1981, 184.

8. Barry Kosmin, Sidney Goldstein, et al., *Highlights of the CJF 1990 National Jewish Population Survey*, Council of Jewish Federations, New York, 1991.

9. Bernard Wasserstein, *Vanishing Diaspora*, Hamish Hamilton, London, 1996; Alan M. Dershowitz, *The Vanishing American Jew*, Boston, Little, Brown, 1997.

10. Genesis 24:3.

11. Genesis 26:34–5; 27:46.
12. Deuteronomy 7:3.
13. Ezra 10:2; Nehemiah 13:23–28
14. Babylonian Talmud, *Avodah Zarah* 31b, 35b.
15. Egon Mayer, *Love and Tradition*, Schocken Books, New York, 1987, 48.
16. Jonathan Sacks, *Will We Have Jewish Grandchildren?*, Vallentine Mitchell, London, 1994.
17. Edmund Fleg, *Why I Am a Jew*, trans. Victor Gollancz, Gollancz, London, 1943, 7.
18. Numbers 23:9.
19. Elliott Abrams, *Faith or Fear*, The Free Press, New York, 1997, 127.
20. Seymour Lipset and Earl Raab, *Jews and the New American Scene*, Harvard University Press, Cambridge, 1995, 61.

CHAPTER 15: THIS IS OURS

1. Genesis 32:25–29.
2. Genesis 27:28.
3. Genesis 28:3–4.
4. John Murray Cuddihy, *The Ordeal of Civility: Freud, Marx, Levi-Strauss and the Jewish Struggle with Modernity*, Beacon, Boston, 1987, 48. See also Yosef Hayim Yerushalmi, *Freud's Moses: Judaism Terminable and Interminable*, Yale University Press, New Haven, 1991.
5. In conversation.
6. Shakespeare, *Sonnets*, 29; T. S. Eliot, *Ash Wednesday*, I, line 4.

CHAPTER 16: WHY I AM A JEW

1. Quoted in Geoffrey Wheatcroft, *The Controversy of Zion*, Sinclair-Stevenson, London, 1996, XI.
2. Albert Einstein, "Jewish Ideals," in *Modern Jewish Thought: A Source Reader*, ed. Nahum Glatzer, Schocken Books, New York, 1977, 116.
3. Lewis Carroll, *Through the Looking Glass*, ch. 5.

4. Abraham J. Twerski, *Generation to Generation*, Traditional Press, New York, 1989, 20–21.
5. Joseph B. Soloveitchik, *Halakhic Man*, trans. Lawrence Kaplan, Jewish Publication Society of America, Philadelphia, 1983, 91.
6. *Encyclopaedia Judaica*, vol. 15, 129.
7. *Los Angeles Times*, "Israel and the Palestinian Problem," study no. 149, 1988.
8. Mishnah, *Avot* 1:14.
9. William Safire, *The First Dissident: The Book of Job in Today's Politics*, Random House, New York, 1992, 226.
10. Alasdair MacIntyre, *Against the Self-Images of the Age*, Duckworth, London, 1971, 12–13.
11. G. K. Chesterton, *What I Saw in America*, Da Capo Press, New York, 1968, 7.

Acknowledgments

My THANKS TO the Jewish students who, as I describe in the Prologue, set me thinking about Jewish identity in the modern world, and to the Hong Kong Jewish community, on whom I first tried out some of the ideas in this book.

No one could have had two more delightful people to work with than Alys Yablon, my editor at The Free Press, and Louise Greenberg, my literary agent. Together they helped me wrestle the text into coherence, and whatever merits it has is largely due to their tactful and ever-patient perfectionism.

As with all I do, I owe a large debt of thanks to my wonderful office team: Malcolm Lachs, Syma Weinberg, Jeremy Newmark, Alan Greenbatt, Yael Jackson, Paula Pitts, Joanna Benarroch, Marion Silverstone, Lilian Isaacs, Lara Kallenberg and Rabbi Dr. Julian Shindler. Daily and without complaint, they have shared the burdens of the Chief Rabbinate and made these years a pleasure and privilege.

I recall too, with a deep sense of gratitude, the people who helped me on my own Jewish journey: the late Rabbi Menachem Mendel Schneersohn, the Lubavitcher Rebbe, and Rabbi Joseph Soloveitchik, both of blessed memory;

and Rabbi Nachum Rabinovitch, my teacher and mentor for twelve years.

More than with any other book I have written, while writing this I held constantly in mind our children, Joshua, Dina and Gila, and our daughter-in-law Eve. Psalm 127 calls children "God's heritage and reward," and I thank Him daily for ours. By the time the book is published, Elaine and I will, God willing, have celebrated our thirtieth wedding anniversary. We married young, long before I thought of becoming a rabbi, and through those years she has been the joy of my life. Nothing I have done could I have done without her.

Ultimately, this book is a token of thanks to my mother (may she have many more years of health) and my late father. My father was a simple man who lived by simple truths. He had a hard life; he came to the West as a child fleeing from persecution, and he had to leave school at the age of fourteen to support his family. When I was young, I used to ask him many questions about Judaism, and his answer was always the same. "Jonathan," he used to say, "I didn't have an education, and so I do not know the answers to your questions. But one day you will have the education I missed, and then you will teach me the answers." Could anyone have been given a greater gift than that? He was a proud Jew, and he wanted his children to go further than he could, along the path of faith. My three brothers, Brian, Alan, and Eliot, and I have tried in our different ways to do just that, and I dedicate this book to his memory.

Index